Social Movements in Iran

Despite the growing significance of social movements worldwide, scholarship on the subject remains largely Western in nature, with studies written primarily by Western scholars and based on the experiences of Western cultures and societies. This book makes an important contribution to the study of social movements in non-Western societies by examining their development in Iran. With a particular focus on the recent environmental movement, the author sheds new light on the implications and significance of these movements.

Drawing on in-depth original research, the case study of the environmental movement is integrated into a historical and comparative analysis. Implementing the new social movement theory of Touraine and Melucci in the Iranian context, the author shows that although the reform movement of Iran is unique, in some aspects it is a continuation of the past social movements. She places emphasis on the role of women in recent Iranian social movements, exploring the significance of social movements in civil society and in instigating social change.

Using the case of Iran to offer a critical framework for studying social change and transformation of non-European countries, this book fills an important gap in the existing literature on the topic. As such, it will be of great interest to scholars and students of sociology, political science and Middle Eastern studies.

Simin Fadaee is Assistant Professor for the sociology of Asia and Africa at Humboldt University Berlin. Her research interests lie in the areas of social movements, social inequality, globalization and social structure.

Iranian Studies

Edited by:
Homa Katouzian, University of Oxford and Mohamad Tavakoli, University of Toronto.

Since 1967 the International Society for Iranian Studies (ISIS) has been a leading learned society for the advancement of new approaches in the study of Iranian society, history, culture, and literature. The new ISIS Iranian Studies series published by Routledge will provide a venue for the publication of original and innovative scholarly works in all areas of Iranian and Persianate Studies.

Social Movements in Iran

Environmentalism and civil society

Simin Fadaee

Routledge
Taylor & Francis Group

LONDON AND NEW YORK

First published 2012
by Routledge
2 Park Square, Milton Park, Abingdon, Oxon OX14 4RN

Simultaneously published in the USA and Canada
by Routledge
711 Third Avenue, New York, NY 10016

*Routledge is an imprint of the Taylor & Francis Group, an informa
business*

British Library Cataloguing in Publication Data
A catalogue record for this book is available from the British
Library

Library of Congress Cataloging in Publication Data
Fadaee, Simin.
  Social movements in Iran : environmentalism and civil society /
Simin Fadaee.
     p. cm. – (Iranian studies)
  Includes bibliographical references and index.
  1. Environmentalism–Iran. 2. Social movements–Iran. I. Title.
  GE199.I7F33 2012
  303.48'40955–dc23
             2011036410

ISBN 978-0-415-69357-8 (hbk)
ISBN 978-0-203-12690-5 (ebk)

Typeset in Times New Roman
by Taylor & Francis Books

Printed and bound in the United States of America
by Edwards Brothers Malloy, Inc.

Contents

Illustrations

Figures

Table

Preface

Social movements have changed, and more than ever continue to change, the landscape of our globalizing world in different ways. However, shortage of academic analysis on the dynamics of social movements and change in general, and in non-Western contexts in particular, has made the systematic analysis of these complex collective actions complicated, and in some cases impossible. By applying new social movement theory to the Iranian context, unlike most other publications on Iran that ignore the embodied Euro-centrism of sociological theory, this book offers a critical framework for better understanding social change and transformation in the non-Western context. Moreover, by offering an original in-depth study of Iranian environmentalism, it provides readers with an insight into one of the most novel and important, but neglected, aspects of contemporary Iranian civil society and social movements. Therefore, the book is essentially an introduction to a book that might be written in future—sociology of social movements in Iran.

The book is intended for students of social movements, and Iranian and Middle Eastern studies. However, readers unfamiliar with social science and the Middle East should also find the book understandable and not too complicated. Moreover, it could be of use to social activists and political scientists. In general, anyone with a serious interest in Iran and sociology could find some interesting information in the following pages.

Acknowledgments

Being an Iranian and having lived in Iran for most of my life, I have always been inspired by the people of Iran; who despite pain, anxiety, and frustration, never give up their battle against injustice and repression. For the greater part of their history, imprisonment, torture, and death have been part of daily life for Iranians. Nonetheless, these fearless women and men, with tears and laughter, insistence and patience, combat the pains, hoping for a brighter tomorrow. I dedicate this book to the people of Iran and their continuous struggle for change.

Publication of this book would not have been possible without the enormous help and assistance of many individuals and institutions. Prof. Boike Rehbein has been the main source of academic inspiration and support for me. I express my utmost gratitude to him. Additionally, I am grateful to Prof. Hermann Schwengel for his constant help and critique. Prof. Ari Sitas and Prof. Alireza Dehghan have encouraged me enormously from the early years of my academic awakening. I wish to express my great gratitude to them. The entire manuscript has been read and commented on by Seth Schindler. I express my special thanks to him. I am thankful to the International Graduate Academy (IGA) of the Albert-Ludwigs University of Freiburg for their financial support.

I would also like to thank the countless Iranian individuals (specifically environmental activists) and institutions, who assisted me during my research. Without their kind help and cooperation this study would not have been feasible. It is impossible to name the huge number of my friends, in Germany, Iran, and all over the globe, whose friendship and loyalty (despite long distances in many cases) have contributed to this work in different ways. My brother Arman has always been there for me. Although I am supposed to be his older sister, his profound insight and deep emotions have, on many occasions, made me the little sister, learning from him.

Above all, I would like to express my greatest gratitude to my parents Ashraf Amini and Shareef Fadaee, who have always supported me with their love and attention. From them I have learned things no book, school, or university could have taught me. They are my best teachers and friends, and there are no words to thank them for all the support they have provided throughout the years. Their sacrifice made this moment possible.

Introduction

Social movements have been considered by many sociologists to be one of the main agents of social transformation. The idea of social movements as agents of historical change can be seen in different variations in the work of many scholars such as Touraine (1981), Habermas (1992), and Offe (1984). The emergence, dynamics, and development of social movements can signal transformation processes of societies. The movements themselves can be seen as indicators of society's circumstances, and capable of affecting structural changes in the social and political realms.

In the twentieth century, three important events contributed to the significance of social movement studies. First, the two world wars, and the rise of the fascist and communist movements; second, the dissolution of the colonial world, and the emergence of various numbers of social movements; and third, the acceleration of the globalization process, and the consequent rise of transnational social movements. In the present context of globalization, in which political, social, and cultural changes are rapidly occurring, the study of social movements and their transformations have gained special importance (see Eyerman and Jamison 1991).

Anthony Giddens, in *Social theory and Modern Sociology* (1987: 48), claimed that "social movements will continue to be of prime significance in stimulating the sociological imagination." In *The Consequences of Modernity*, he argued that "social movements provide significant guidelines to potential future transformations" (Giddens 1990: 158). Giddens believes that social movements reflect on the four basic institutional dimensions of modernity and their interrelations, that is capitalism (capital accumulation in the context of competitive labor and product markets), surveillance (control of information and social supervision), military power (control of the means of violence in the context of the industrialization of war), and industrialism (transformation of nature: development of the created environment) (Giddens 1990). Some scholars emphasize the many developments (recent and non-recent) within social sciences and the structural changes as a response to the activities of social movements. (Scott 1990: 1)

Despite the growing significance of social movements worldwide, especially the emergence of transnational social movements, the problem remains the Western nature of the studies and existing theories in this area. These studies and theories, mostly written by Western scholars, are usually based on the experiences of their own societies. Marxists provide a class-based analysis of social movements and locate them between class and labor. New social movement theory emphasizes the post-materialist conditions of post-modern or programmed society, in which the focus is towards identity formation. However, theoretical or empirical studies on the social movements of the Global South are rare. This has resulted in a failure of understanding the nature of social movements in non-Western contexts; being either completely ignorant about them or failing to give a true explanation about their reality. That is why the importance of diverse and crucial non-European social movements, their implications, and the significance of these societies in world development, have not received enough attention.

This study seeks to implement the new social movement theory of Touraine and Melucci in the Iranian context. In explaining the rise of new social movements, this theory pays considerable attention to the social structures of the post-modern era, seeing European modernity as a prerequisite of the new society (i.e. "programmed" or "complex" society). This conceptualization of society and social structure ignores the cultural and historical traditions of non-European societies and their importance in shaping contemporary world order. Firstly, such negligence ignores the fact that although European modernity at a time of European renaissance became the main advocator of "modernity," world history is much older than the history of European Enlightenment. Therefore instead of referring to "modernity," we should be talking about "multiple modernities" (Eisenstadt 2003). Secondly, such assumptions not only ignore the importance of the historical traditions of non-European civilizations, but take the mutual interaction of "multiple modernities" in the process of globalization for granted (Eisenstadt 2004). If modernity varies across societies and civilizations, the nature of (new) social movements should also differ in different contexts.

This book is concerned with social movements in Iran from the start of the twentieth century onwards. However, my main focus is on the newly emerged environmental movement, in order to provide an understanding of the dynamics and potential of contemporary social movements in Iran. The choice of environmentalism reflects several factors: firstly, more than anything, environmental movements, along with the feminism and human rights movements, have been among the most prominent movements of the "new social movement" paradigm. This makes the application of the "new social movement" theory in the Iranian case more feasible. Secondly, environmental damage under the Islamic regime has been extremely serious and has directly affected many segments of Iranian society. Thirdly, environmentalism is usually regarded as a Western phenomenon, but it has recently gained popularity in the non-Western context. Finally, environmentalism is today one of the most important global issues.

Most recent studies of Iranian society have neglected grassroots struggles, oppositional groups, and social movements, and have instead focused on the regime's policies and governmental institutions. I am mostly interested in presenting insights on Iranian social movements as a form of social life, something that has not gained enough attention in literature on studies of Iranian society.

Two revolutionary movements within one century (i.e. the 1905–6 constitutional revolution and the 1979 Islamic revolution), an 8-year war (1981–9), and globalization have significantly contributed to the distinctive nature of contemporary Iranian society. This makes it an attractive subject for investigation in general, and particularly the case of social movements and their transformation. However, an explanation for the rise, growth, and fall of social movements within this sociopolitical context requires study of the specificity of history, social structure, and forms of mobilization.

Since the early twentieth century, Iran has experienced different stages of social movement uprising. Each stage faced a special form of a social movement, as every social structure creates its own types of protest and movement. During the Qajar government, interference by Britain and Russia in Iranian political life, as well as the challenges posed by a traditional government, were at the forefront of problems for Iranians. Also, Iranian society has been exposed to new ideas through modernization and contact with the West. As a result, in a collective action the people aimed to change the traditional political system through a constitution and a parliament. In reaction to the hegemonic power of the British on the internal resources of the country, Iranians supported Mosaddegh's nationalist movement in 1951–3, which led to the nationalization of the oil industry. Being confronted with the dependence of the Shah on US policies, and the rapid Westernization of the country, many groups (mainly communists, nationalists, and Islamists) aimed to overthrow the government. This was followed by the Islamic Republic. About a decade ago, society gave birth to the reform movement, which advocates the ideas of civil society and citizenship rights. This move-ment has provided a base for the emergence of many other social movements, including environmental movements.

In 1997, a set of political and social reforms were launched, starting with the presidential election and moving to numerous other institu-tions, such as city councils, governmental organs, universities, etc. In the aftermath of these changes, society went through some fundamental changes and a new set of social movements emerged. Movements within this context were mainly directed at political change, but also contained in many cultural and social aspects, which are not irre-ducible to politics. Transformation of life styles, the changed role of media, and new individual demands, which gained a rapid pace in the 1990s, all contributed to a profound change in Iranian culture and everyday life. That is why, besides focusing on political dimensions, we need to pay special attention to the sociocultural transformations of the society during recent years. However, this does not mean the impact and political importance of these transformations is minimal, rather to emphasize that a purely political reading of them would fail to under-stand the innovative nature of the changes that occurred. Furthermore, it would ignore the fact that the politics itself is shifting to another domain.

The main argument in this study describes the rise of a set of actions, or in sociological terms, social movements, which are "new" in nature. However, there are few scientific studies of these newly emerged movements. Thus, their essence and nature remains unknown. As "newness" is a relative concept, which functions initially to emphasize some comparative differences between the previous forms of action/structure and the contemporary forms, I intend to study the con-temporary movements in comparison with older forms of social movements. Characters and essence of the previous movements have been sketched in order to serve as background and comparison to the new movements.

In his study of modern social movements in Iran, Poulson (2006) argues that there has been a cyclical rise of social movements in Iran during the twentieth century. With a brief overview of the nature of these movements, I intend to cite the argument that Poulson defends, in which he believes that there has been a continuation in the life of Iranian social movements during the twentieth century. However, one main question remains unanswered: are the social movements that emerged during the last decade a continuation of previous social movements or "new" kinds of social movements? Raising arguments on the notability of these movements, alongside scientific inquiry to reveal the unknown character of these forms of action, are the main concerns in this study.

Using the Touraine/Melucci model as a basis for theoretical analysis, the main argument is that environmental movements are among the "new" social movements in Iran, and they are notably different from past movements of modern era. Contrary to the beliefs of mainstream academicians, the new movements have some of the characteristics of their European counterparts, but at the same time have their own specific natures. What is notable about the new movements, and to what extent the Touraine/Melucci model is capable of explaining their reality in the Iranian context, is argued throughout the whole of this book, and especially the concluding chapters.

This book starts from the first organized Iranian social movements of the twentieth century, which marks the beginning of the modern era, and moves to the contemporary epoch. It explores the most remarkable forms of social movements of this period. Special attention has been paid to the political history of the mentioned era, its modernization process, and consequent societal changes. Although the environmental movement in itself is a small-scale movement in comparison with the four mass movements that took place in Iran in the twentieth century (that is, the constitutional, national oil, 1979 revolutionary and reform movements), it provides an important case for explaining the "newness" of recent forms of collective action. However, the non-nationwide character of the environmental movement is, in itself, an explanation of emergence of a new kind of social movement that differs from its older partners.

Three interrelated objectives have been identified in this study. One was to explore how modern social movements developed in Iranian society. In order to come to a meaningful understanding of the present, we have to understand the past; to analyze past and present, to see if there is any continuity in the life of the social movements, and to examine the extent to which the past has influenced the present forms of social movements.

Furthermore, as Barington Moore's (1966) study on the social origins of dictatorship and democracy has shown us, we should avoid forcing histories of any kind into already existing theories. In other words, different societies have their own lines of history, which can enrich the task of theory building.

Charles Tilly (2004: 3) argues that social movements require historical understanding. Firstly, because history provides a framework for understanding why social movements have followed specific patterns in the past. Secondly, history helps us explain momentous changes in social movements, and, therefore, highlights possible changes for the future. Thirdly, history draws our attention to the shifting socio-political conditions that give rise to social movements. An overview of the social movements of the twentieth century, which marks the beginning of the Iranian new modern era, has contributed to this aim. Because of the constraints of resources and time, I have dealt only with the most prominent social movements of the twentieth century. However, this does not undermine the importance of other social movements, which did not gain a mass following.

The second aim was to offer an overview of the environmental movement in Iranian society as an example of a contemporary movement. This helps us inquire into the circumstances that influenced the emergence and dynamics of the movement. Understanding the forces and challenges of the environmental movement is crucial in order to explain shifts in Iranian cultural, social, and political attitudes in general.

The final aim was to examine the relevance of "new social movement theory," namely the Touraine/Melucci model, which is one of the most important models of new social movement theory, in a non-Western context, that is Iranian society. Besides, as the nature of civil society and the newly emerged social movements are interconnected, the research advances two more sets of findings: on the nature and development of civil society in contemporary Iran, and the implications of the rise of civil society for the state and social movements. The rest of this book pursues the following structure.

Chapter 1 provides an outline of the concept of the social movement. It also offers a theoretical framework for further analysis of current Iranian social movements. The Touraine/Melucci model, which is the theoretical approach adopted in this study is summarized and introduced. By shedding brief light on some aspects of Iranian history and social structure, the chapter concludes that the Touraine/Melucci approach, with its focus on European history, modernity, and social structure, is inadequate for a proper understanding of social phenomena (or the specific case of social movements) in Iran, and other non-European societies. However, this will be argued in detail in Chapter 5 of the book. Chapters 2, 3 and 4 provide a historical and empirical background for Chapter 5.

Chapter 2 offers an overview of the four prominent social movements in Iran in the twentieth century. It starts from the constitutional movement of 1905–6, then describes the movement for nationalization of the country's oil, the revolutionary movement of 1979, and, finally, the recent reform movement. The chapter claims that there has been continuity and a meaningful dynamic in the life of Iranian social movements in the twentieth century. However, the reform movement has prominent differences from the previous social movements. The final conclusion of the chapter claims that, with the rise of the reform movement, society had undergone deep transformations. These changes led to the emergence of new sets of actors and social actions, including environmental movements.

Chapter 3 is a detailed account of the changes that occurred in the political and social discourse of Iranian society in the aftermath of the reform movement. The nature and development of civil society in Iran, and its present situation is briefly explained. It is argued that the emergence of the civil society discourse led to new state–society relationships. New discourses, narratives, counternarratives, and forms of resistance have, in consequence, emerged. However, the presidential election of 2005 and dominance of anti-civil society discourse has brought some changes in the public sphere, leading to a slowing down of civil activities. Nonetheless, the occurred structural changes have brought up new quests for change and reform. This quest has become part of the present and future of the Iranian society (as we can see in the present pro-democracy movement of Iranians known as the Green Movement).

Chapter 4, which is the case study of this book, presents the environmental movement in Iran by referring to a selection of environmental groups centered in Tehran and Rasht, in order to present groups operating at the center and the periphery of the movement. The environmental groups are presented according to their focus on the issue of environment, but their aims and goals, activities, participants, challenges and the degree of achievement, and their current status are also explored.

In Chapter 5, I link the theory with empirical findings in order to examine the relevance of the Touraine/Melucci model in the Iranian context, and to explore to what extent Touraine/Melucci's arguments are applicable in Iran. This includes considerations of the concepts of modernity, civil society, and (new) social movements as has been discussed in new social movement theory. It is shown that the Touraine/Melucci model has some relevance in the Iranian context. However, its reliance on European social structure and history makes it inadequate to explain some aspects of Iranian society. The chapter ends with a brief outline of possible considerations, which might lead to a more adequate model.

In the final chapter, I portray an overall conclusion to the study by comparing its achievements with its objectives. Moreover, I discuss the inadequacy of social movement studies specifically, and sociological study in general, in the Iranian context.

Methodology

This study is sociological and historical. It is sociological because it aims to investigate the nature of the Iranian social movements and, consequently, social structures. It is historical because it deals with changes in Iranian social movements that have occurred since the 1900s until the present. To put it differently, it is concerned with the history of modern social movements in Iran.

This combination not only helps us to understand what happened in the past, but also allows us to explore how society has changed, and how present society is different from the past. Moreover, it allows us to explore the changes and the continuities, as well as the distinctive and shared characteristics, of the present society with the past. This helps to understand why the contemporary movements have emerged and why they are different from previous movements. In order to be able to do this, the focus is mainly on four elements: the state–society relationship, causes of the movements, the social actors and their identity, and the process of mobilization (modes of association) and achievements of each movement. The case of the environmental movement as an ongoing contemporary movement has been elaborated in detail.

Because of the nature of the task, this study is based on two distinct kinds of resources: firstly, historical texts, which have helped me explore the essence of the past movements; secondly, empirical research, which was carried out on current environmental movements in Iran.

The empirical research for this book was conducted in two phases: between July and September 2007 and in October 2008. During my first phase of research I was confronted with the fact that many of the environmental groups are centered in Tehran, representing the dominance of the Iranian capital. However, these organizations have many branches in different parts of the country. I found out that apart from the Tehran-centered branches, each region contains many local groups, which undertake quite different activities and have a different orientation in comparison with Tehran. Further investigation brought me to the assumption that the movement has a core (Tehran) with different peripheral hubs. However, each peripheral hub has its own peripheries. Furthermore, because of the loose structure of the movement, the hubs and peripheries cannot be distinguished clearly. As time was limited, I decided to draw my focus on the environmental groups of Tehran (core) and one of the peripheral hubs as an example of the periphery. This combination was chosen in order to address two important issues: firstly, to provide a more comprehensive study of the movements' nature by avoiding presentation of a homogeneous character of movements, and, secondly, to bring the voices of the activists on the periphery into my work. This has been important in decreasing the dominance of Tehran as the center. However, my aim was not to present any representative of the periphery here, as the time constraints and the diversity of the groups make this an almost impossible task. Therefore, I find it important to emphasize that this choice is just an example of what can be called the periphery of the movement and it does not represent the diversity of the periphery.

With respect to the activities of all other environmental groups in different regions of Iran, I decided to choose Rasht (the center of the northern province Gilan) as an example of the peripheral hub. Due to the numerous interesting works of all other regions, this task has been one of the most challenging aspects of my work. However, the choice of Rasht reflects a few important factors. Firstly, sociocultural contacts with Russia during the centuries have made the northern provinces of Iran relatively open and least conservative. This factor was taken into account before choosing the peripheral region, because the relative willingness of people to be open about their issues is a fundamental part of any kind of social study. Concerning the current political situation in Iran, without the appreciable assistance of the interviewees, any kind of interview with the activists would be impossible. Moreover, as a woman I would not have been very successful in some conservative regions.

Additionally, Northern Iran is known for its mild, moderate, and Mediterranean-like climate, which along with the Caspian Sea and the outstanding forestry regions (which are unique in the dry and mountainous landscape of Iran) and proximity to Tehran have made the north one of the main tourist areas. Although tourism has brought the region a relative amount of wealth, it has also destroyed large portions of its natural environment. Indeed, this region is one of the most environmentally damaged locations in the country, explaining why the sensibility of the inhabitants of this region towards their natural environment is very high. This has given rise to the outstanding growth of environmental organizations in the northern provinces.

Furthermore, as Rasht is the largest city along the Caspian Sea coast (provinces of Gilan, Mazandaran, and Golestan), many environmental organizations are located in this city. At the same time Rasht, with a population of around 600,000 is an intermediate city in demographical categorizations of Iranian cities, which makes it a good (periphery) case to be compared with the (core) Tehran (around 12 million).

My first task during data collection was identification of environmental groups and their contact information. Through my online research, I compiled a list of environmental non-governmental organizations (NGOs) and their contact persons through the official website of the Iranian Department of Environment. After reviewing the list, I started contacting each group, requesting an interview with representatives when possible. Surprisingly, many of the mentioned organizations were no longer active, although their names and contact numbers were on the list of the Department of Environment. What surprised me more was that, through the other NGOs I was introduced to a number of new groups, which were not on the given list. After conducting an interview with the head of the Participation and Public Education Bureau in the Iranian Department of Environment, it became clear that the list is not comprehensive. Apparently, after the restructuring of the Department of Environment following the presidential election of 2005, there were some policy changes regarding collaboration of the department and NGOs, which reduced the collaboration to a very low level. This could explain the inadequacy of the information.

However, during both phases of my field work, after a few days in the field, through informal connections, I had the names and contact details of most of the active groups. Each group that I contacted introduced me to the others.

A single informed person was interviewed from each NGO. The interviews were based on a semi-structured questionnaire and each lasted between 1 and 2 hours. In most cases, I was welcomed by the organizations. None refused to be interviewed and only one asked for proof of my research. In total, 37 in-depth semi-structured interviews were conducted with top level representatives, the founding member, director, the information officer, or another senior official. In most cases, the interviews were recorded and transcribed, but a few of the activists preferred their voices not to be recorded. The interviews focused on the origin of the groups, their ideology, organizational structure, location within the movement (contact with others and the degree of influence), activities, participants, perception of environmental conditions (problems), and their difficulties and achievements. The interviews not only enabled me to check and re-check facts about the movement, but they also helped me to gain an understanding of the perceptions of the participants towards the facts and issues. These interviews provide the central resource of my case study. The sample reflects different types of groups operating within the movement.

In addition to interviews conducted with NGO representatives, a few interviews were carried out with officials from the Department of Environment and a few civil society activists. Although a lot of time was spent on observation, I also attended a number of workshops and seminars held by the environmental NGOs. This was done to increase my understanding of the groups' approach. Moreover, some informal conversations were held with leaders and activists. An analysis of the documentary materials of each organization such as newsletters, posters, websites, and other relevant material was also taken into account.

However, the given picture of the Iranian environmental movement discloses the movement only at a specific time, when the data were collected. As the environmental movement is a dynamic force that evolves permanently, it will have changed since my data collection. We should, therefore, avoid any kind of static view of the movement. Moreover, as was mentioned before, the peripheral hubs of the environmental movement are diverse and numerous. Choosing a different peripheral hub or hubs other than Rasht, could have contributed to a different understanding of the movement. Thirdly, because of the contentious subject of the study, many questions had to be tackled indirectly or avoided during the interviews. This made the analysis of some aspects of the movement difficult and challenging.

● Tehran

● Rasht

Figure 0.1 Map of Iran

1 Theoretical framework

Introduction

This chapter aims to clarify two important issues of the study. The first aim is to explain the meaning of a social movement as a kind of collective action. A collective action is a multi-layer social action, which carries different characteristics in the course of time and space. In order to distinguish a social movement from a similar kind of collective action, it is necessary to clarify the meaning of the concept of a "social movement."

The second objective of this chapter is to introduce the Touraine/Melucci model, which is one of the key models of the new social movement theory. My intention here is to elaborate on this model, in order to provide a framework for further analysis on the relevance of the Touraine/Melucci model in a non-European context. The final section of this chapter provides an introduction to this discussion. Further in-depth analysis will be provided in the concluding chapters of the study.

What is a social movement?

A social movement is a kind of collective behavior. "The collective behavior refers to the behavior of two or more individuals who are acting together or collectively" (Smelser 1962: 3). In other words, "collective behavior is the behavior of individuals under the influence of an impulse that is common and collective, an impulse, which is the result of social interaction" (Park 1967: 226).

There are different kinds of collective behavior. Social movements are similar to "political parties" and "interest groups." Thus, to clarify the meaning of the term "social movement," I first try to distinguish it from these two terms.

As defined by the *International Encyclopedia of the Social and Behavioral Sciences* (Smelser and Baltes 2001), social movements are collective behaviors acting outside institutional channels aiming for or against change in an institution or the society. In contrast, political parties are groups of people, labeled as "Republican," "Labor," etc.— labels generally applied by themselves and others. The rights of the political party to promote their objectives are guaranteed by law in many countries, and, moreover, political parties sometimes opt for governmental representation through nominations and elections.

Interest groups are organizations, ranging from business and professional associations to labor unions to environmental and consumer groups and many other groups working on different issues. Their main task is building a bridge between individuals and public institutions in order to influence public policy. In most cases interest groups are directly or indirectly connected to political parties and social movements (Smelser and Baltes 2001).

Referring to the above explanations provided by the *International Encyclopedia of the Social and Behavioral Sciences*, we could differentiate a social movement from a political party in that social movement activism is rarely concerned with nomination of a person for any political position, although there are political parties that support certain social movements. Moreover, unlike political parties, the goals and strategies of a social movement are not always recognized by the wider society. Social movements also can be distinguished from interest groups by their lesser degree of organization. Even though social movements have some level of organization, when compared with interest groups, members of social movements can much more easily leave the movement without any formalities. Moreover, a social movement comprises different kinds of formal and informal groups, organizations, media, etc.

I propose the following definition as a basis for understanding of social movements: a social movement can be referred to as a system of collective action, by a group of people who are consciously aiming for or against a particular change in other people, structures, or relations. Social movements follow a level of organization, that is they are more organized than mobs or crowds, but less organized than formal and bureaucratic organizations.

How can the emergence and dynamics of a social movement be explained?

Although protests against inequality, tyranny, and repression have occurred throughout human history, social movements, as they are known today, are a product of recent history. In the late eighteenth and early nineteenth centuries, industrialization and consequent changes in agriculture, manufacturing, and transportation had a profound effect on socioeconomic and cultural conditions in Europe, and later on, in the rest of the world. The polarization of the society into proletariat and bourgeoisie, which went hand-in-hand with an epistemological shift in Europe, led to the emergence of the labor movements of the eighteenth and nineteenth centuries. Later on, as a response to Western forces of colonization, the nationalist and anti-colonialist movements of the first half of the twentieth century emerged.

The most dominant analysis of the social movements in this period was related to the class struggle and Marxist analysis of the labor movement. In this analysis, society consists of different classes. The process of industrialization brought the two important classes of society, the bourgeoisie (the owners of the means of the production, the factories, and the land), and the proletariat (the working class who perform the necessary labor for the extraction of the necessary value from the means of production), into conflict. This conflict was the basis for the emergence of social movements. As industrial society developed, this conflict grew. On the one hand, the bourgeoisie exploited the proletariat workforce, to produce and accumulate more; on the other hand, the number of poor proletariats increased. The impetus for development of social movement in this period was "class consciousnesses." Class consciousness united the proletariat against the capitalist system and bourgeoisie. So, class discrimination and class consciousness were two bases for the emergence of social movements over this period of time, as was explained by the Marxist theorists.

In the middle of the twentieth century, however, the communist and fascist movements were changing the political order of Europe and as a result social movements became an important topic for European sociologists. It was assumed that gaining knowledge of such movements would help social scientists analyzing the potential of social movements to change established society. The emergence of the collective behavior paradigm was a sociological response to the political context of the rise of fascism in Europe (Eyerman and Jamison 1991: 10).

Herbert Blumer, one of the main theorists of the collective behavior paradigm, was a "symbolic interactionist." In explaining the emergence and rise of collective behaviors, his focus was on the emergent norms, processes of self-regulation, social creativity, and internal reforms (Blumer 1951; Eyerman and Jamison 1991).

On the other hand, Parsons, another theorist of the collective behavior paradigm, had a "structural functionalist" approach. His focus was on the social determinism embodied in collective behavior, and the social strains that influenced the formation of collective behavior (Eyerman and Jamison 1991: 13). In his analysis of the fascist movement, Parsons calls fascism, "the most dramatic single development in the society of the western world which is deeply rooted in the structure of western society and its internal trends and conflicts" (Parsons 1982: 124). Being influenced by the ideas of Emile Durkheim, Parsons believed that human actions are symbolic and intentional, but that they are defined within a framework of complex systems of interrelated sub-systems (see Parsons 1967, 1951). Moreover, he assumed that it is possible to apply the definition of action to a system of actions. At this level of analysis, individual personalities are no longer the unit of analysis, and instead existing relations between actors at the level of social systems are analyzed (Parsons and Shills 1951). In general, collective behavior theorists pay special attention to individuals, their stories and motivations, personal biographies, and institutional as well as personal changes in order to explain and analyze social movements (see Eyerman and Jamison 1991).

While the expansion of the state as a central coordinating mechanism in society was changing the sociopolitical atmosphere of both Europe and America, the essential difference in the character of the social forces leading to this state expansion directly affected the way social movements were understood and analyzed by Western sociologists (Eyerman and Jamison 1991). For example, the student movements of the 1960s were particularly shocking phenomena for sociologists because the already existing theories, that is the symbolic interactionism and structural functionalist approaches of the collective behavior paradigm, were unable to explain the rise of such kinds of social movements at the universities. Before the uprisings of the 1960s, universities were assumed to be some of the most integrated modern institutions. Moreover, the students were assume to be one of the most adjusted social groups, neither deviants nor outcasts. Therefore, the collective behavior approach (neither symbolic interactionist nor structural functionalist) could not explain why students were attracted to protests and disruptive behaviors at the university. Also, the Marxist approach, with its focus on relations of production and its class analysis, was unable to explain the phenomena of student movements (Eyerman and Jamison 1991: 17).

In general, following the social unrests of the 1960s and the post-war decade, two different trends were occurring in the study of social movements in the USA and Europe. In post-1960s USA, the "resource mobilization paradigm" was emerging as a challenge to the collective behavior approach (see Eyerman and Jamison 1991; Morris and Herring 1987). Unlike the collective behavior approach, which views social movements as deviants, resource mobilization theorists believe that social movements are formed by rational social institutions and social actors. The theorists of this approach explain the origins of social movements by linking them to the existence of grievances in a society. Furthermore, they emphasize that grievances alone are not sufficient conditions for the rise of social movements. The availability of resources and opportunities for shaping a collective action count as the most important factor, which leads the individuals to make collective political demands (see McCarthy and Zald 1973; Zald and McCarthy 1988).

The main thesis of this approach is that the formation of social movements is a conscious and organized act, and it assumes that individuals are rational beings. Social movements are therefore goal-oriented activities. Individuals are thus viewed as calculators of the costs and benefits of the movement. Resource mobilization theory analyzes social movement activity as purposeful and rational behavior. Whereas social movement participation was basically thought of as spontaneous and irrational by previous theorists, it is analyzed as both conscious and rational within the resource mobilization theory (Zald and McCarthy 1988: 11). As is inferred from the name, the resource mobilization approach emphasizes the variety of resources that should be mobilized in a social movement, such as relations of the social movements to other groups, the external supports on which social movements rely, and the tactics used by authorities to control or incorporate movements (Zald and McCarthy 1988: 16).

Similar to any other paradigm, the resource mobilization paradigm rests on a variety of thoughts. Charles Tilly (1984) focuses on the relation of collective action, and the broad changes in political structure. Anthony Oberschall (1973) and Bert Klandermans (1988) link expectations of success to the number of people participating in a movement. They put more emphasis on the analysis of the relations between individuals, and the factors leading to participation of social movement activists from a micro perspective. Doug Macadam (1982) emphasizes the political aspects of mobilization, focusing on how opportunities for social movement action are being shaped through different regime policies.

At a time when North American sociologists were focused on the "resource mobilization theory," in Europe, the term "new social movement" was introduced as an explanation for the emergence of activities concerned with issues regarding women, the environment, human rights, homo-sexuality, etc. The term "new social movement" was established to make a distinction between the new movements and the old institutionalized movements of the working class. The distinction referred to fundamental shifts in social structure, and the emergence of a new kind of society, i.e. post-industrial society. New social movement theory emphasized that there is something "historically new" in the recent movements, which makes them different from the movements of the past, which belonged to another historical epoch. In contrast to the Marxist analysis of social movements, new social movement theorists are less concerned with economic issues; rather, they are concentrated on issues related to quality of life. The attentions of the new social movement theorists are directed at understanding the essence of these new movements within the form-work of post-industrial society and the structural shift from industrial society.

The characteristics of these new movements have been summarized in different ways. Firstly, the new movements adhere to new values, i.e. the participants in these movements desire new relations to nature, to their own body, to the opposite sex, to work, to consumption patterns, etc. The new movements are mainly concerned with the question of culture and seek new life-styles. Their main focus is on identity and symbols while challenging the older values. Secondly, the new movements carry different forms and actions; however, they are mostly small scale, anti-hierarchical and decentralized. Thirdly, the new movements emerge as extra-institutional phenomena, being contextualized within the sphere of civil society. To use Claus Offe's (1980) phrase, the new movements "bypass the state," and are located within civil society. Finally, the new movements try to make a linkage between the cultural (or personal) and political realms. In this regard, they raise issues that were often ignored or underrepresented by the old movements (see e.g. Boggs 1987; Melucci 1980).

In sum, resource mobilization theory focuses on the organization of movements and the mechanisms that encourage participants to join a movement. Further, for resource mobilization theorists, social movement participation is linked to cost-benefits and budgetary calculations. On the other hand, new social movement theory is interested in addressing why and how social movements emerge, linking them to the emergence of new society and its new values and forms of action. In this perspective, society is seen in terms of structures and long-term processes.

Discussions on new social movement theory

The theoretical framework in this study is based on new social move-ment theory, mainly Alain Touraine and Alberto Melucci's social movement theory. Although there are some differences in their per-spectives, Touraine and Melucci's perception of new social movements follows the same line and is considered to be one of the most influential theories within the paradigm of new social movement studies.

The main focus of this model is the question of culture and trans-formation of society from industrial to post-industrial, and how this transformation has influenced social movements. According to this theory, there is a fundamental difference between contemporary movements and the movements of the industrial era, i.e. workers' movements. These differences are explained by referring to structural changes that have occurred in the newly emerged society, which has been referred to as post-industrial, programmed, information or complex society. The "newness" of the "new" movements, therefore, relates to the "new" kind of society and social structures.

Summarizing the huge body of literature on the recent changes is a difficult task. Scholars have made varying contributions to the subject, offering a wide range of literature on the topic. Manuel Castells, in his trilogy, *The Information Age: Economy, Society and Culture*, precisely explained the trends and transformations of the last decades of the twentieth century. In the introduction to the last volume, *End of Millennium*, he writes:

> In the last quarter of the twentieth century, a technological revo-lution, centered around global information, transformed the way we think, we produce, we consume, we trade, we manage, we communicate, we live, we die, we make war, and we make love. A dynamic economy has been constituted around the planet, linking up valuable people and activities from all over the world, while switching off from the networks of power and wealth, people and territories dubbed as irrelevant from the perspective of dominant interests. Space and time, the material foundations of human experience, have been transformed, as the space of flows dominates the space of places, and timeless time supersedes clock time of the industrial era. Expressions of social resistance to the logic of infor-mationalization and globalization build around primary identities, creating defensive communities in the name of God, locality, ethnicity or family. At the same time founding social institutions as impor-tant as patriarchalism and the nation state are called into question

under the combined pressure of globalization of wealth and information, and localization of identity and legitimacy. These processes of structural change include a fundamental transformation of the macro political and macro social contexts that shape and condition social action and human experience around the world.

(Castells 1998: 1)

How and to what extent the new trends have influenced the ways people mobilize themselves through social movements within this new context, have been explained in detail by Touraine and Melucci.

New social movements, subjects of the programmed society: Alain Touraine

Alain Touraine is a French sociologist whose main interest is the study of social movements. His work on "new social movement theory" consists of two levels of analysis: he clarifies and elaborates on the structural dimensions of post-industrial society, the new trends and transformations; and he explains the process of identity construction within a social movement.

Touraine (1995) separates analysis of the society into two levels, i.e. "patterns of development" of a society (diachronic analysis), and its "functioning" (synchronic analysis). He views civil society not only as the ground for, but also the target of, social movements. Whereas the state, system crisis and change are diachronic elements, social relations and the processes of conflict resolution that lead to formation of norms, institutions, and cultural patterns are synchronic. According to Touraine, social movements are concerned with the potentials of cultural patterns of society and, therefore, they are located within the realm of civil society. At the same time, social movements target the components of civil society. According to Touraine, civil society and social movements rise and fall together. Civil society is the field of the public space in which norms, institutions and social relations are positioned (Cohen 1996).

Touraine's analysis of social movements rests on two assumptions: the first emphasizes that "modernity" has given birth to the idea of the "subject." The individual becomes a subject by acting in opposition to the establishments of social domination, in order to produce the "self" freely. However, Touraine sees rationalization and subjectivation as two driving forces of modernity. Touraine's second assumption in analyzing new social movements is that the present society, the "programmed society," has changed structurally from the past society, i.e. industrial society, explaining why the programmed society generates different social movements from those of the industrial society.

The shift in the social movements of the programmed society results from the working class no longer being the center of the social conflict; new forms of societal conflict have emerged. Although the working class has not disappeared, the programmed society has given birth to new kinds of activists such as women activists, students, ecologists, etc. Accordingly, Touraine argues that programmed society is different to industrial society because it has generated these new social movements, which the industrial society could not (did not) generate. These movements are "new" to industrial society. Throughout his work, Touraine claims that in programmed society the central investments are no longer at the level of work organization, as was the case in industrial societies. The focus is changing to cultural meanings. This shift explains the notability of the programmed society, as a new societal type, characterized by new power structures, new forms of domination and new cultural models.

Another significant element of the programmed society according to Touraine is the growing importance of production and accumulation of knowledge, and of educational institutions in the process of social change. Whereas domination in industrial society was linked to the modes and relations of production, in programmed society domination relates to access and control of supply and data processing, which is directed at organizing the social life. This explains why production and distribution of knowledge, medical care, information, education, health and the media, have become centers of programmed society. This is the managerial power in programmed societies, which dominates and articulates opinions, attitudes and actions.

Therefore, in the new society, domination within culture industries is replacing the old forms of domination. In *Critique of Modernity* (Touraine 1995), Touraine explains that programmed society is a place for cultural industries, which have replaced the world of material goods. The cultural components of social relations have gained an important function, and the programmed society is directly linked to the world of values in which new culture and new social relations are being produced. Consequently, the society becomes a network of relations, where forms of behavior and modes of communication play significant roles. Hence, these transformations create a gap between the new culture and society, and the existing foundations of the society. As a result, corresponding to the cultural contents of society becomes a great challenge.

Apart from the concept of programmed society, in order to understand Touraine's sociology of social movements, understanding two interconnected concepts of his sociology is necessary: subject and historicity.

Touraine argues that through mechanisms of learning and political decision making, human societies have the capacity to reproduce, or to adapt to a changing environment. Moreover, they have the capacity not only to develop their own orientations but also the capacity of changing them. They are capable of "generating their objectives and their normativity" (Touraine 1981: 59). It is within this context that the idea of the subject, i.e. "the construction of individuals as actors," becomes the center of Touraine's analysis (Touraine 1981: 59).

In *Critique of Modernity*, Touraine (1995: 232) claims that modernity is neither linked to the technological progress, nor to the growing individualism of human beings. Rather, it is related to the demand for freedom against transformation of individuals into instruments and objects. Rationalization and subjectivation are two faces of modernity in Touraine's arguments. In modern times, rationalization and subjectivation occur at the same time and are two complimentary forces, as are renaissance and reformation. So, modernity can be defined by the existing conflict between the desire of the subject for freedom and the increasingly rational processes encountered by the subject (Touraine 1995).

According to Touraine, in the early years of the modern era, rational laws started to be regarded as governing the world and therefore the human being became the center of the world. The decreasing importance of the meta-social aspects of the world, led to the emergence of human beings who, instead of believing in divine forces, believe in themselves and their actions. Being replaced by the meta-physic forces, the human being started to define himself through mechanisms of invention, resistance, and construction (Touraine 1995).

Touraine tries to reconstruct modernity by placing emphasis on the importance of subjectivation as one crucial element of modernity, in addition to rationality. For him, the process of the human being becoming a subject is the same, with the achievement of rational thought and the ability to resist all kinds of pressures. Therefore, the subject can only be defined in terms of its relationship with rationalization. Touraine believes that rationalization, which flourished as the world lost its divine meanings, made instrumental action possible. The feasibility of instrumental action made the formation of the subject possible because the subject could not exist as long as the world was believed to be ruled by magical forces. The subject, then, is the individual's desire to produce a social environment rather than just consuming it (Touraine 1995). The individual becomes a subject when she/he becomes the creator of meaning, social relations, and change (Touraine 2000).

Touraine (1995: 286–87) believes that it was the modern era that gave individuals the chance for societal action and change. According to him, modernity is the separation of the objectivized world of science and technologies, and the world of subjectivities. This separation made formation of the idea of the subject possible. However, the subject has two faces: on the one hand it is a struggle against dominating apparatuses. On the other, it is defined through respect for the other as subject. Thus, the subject is the active declaration of its freedom while being based on resistance against dominant powers. Furthermore, the subject has a defensive face and an offensive face, which are manifested in the reference to community and desire for personal freedom (Touraine 1995: 296–97).

Touraine (1995) analyzes rationalization and subjectivation in the form of social movements. Resembling the renaissance and the reformation, he argues that modern societies are driven by two conflicting tendencies. One tendency is the creation of naturalist and materialist images of human beings and the world. The other is the discovery of subjectivity, as an opposing force to the ethics of tradition, religion, contemplation, and imitation. The subject will be constituted in self-consciousness and in the struggle against the anti-subject, especially when the apparatuses are culture industries and when they have totalitarian tendency goals. Therefore, Touraine argues that subjectivation is the realm, where rationalization and the interests of the ruling class are in conflict.

Recognition of the other as subject, links subjectivation to social movements. Touraine (1995: 286) believes that social movements are the work of socially defined actors, who, concurrently, fight for a cultural tendency and a hegemonic meaning, but also for a particular social demand or group. Hence, social movements are, simultaneously, a cultural project and a social conflict. If the subject does not become part of a social movement, there is the danger of being driven into individuality. However, "there can be no subject without social commitment and no social movement without a direct appeal to the freedom and responsibility of the subject" (Touraine 1995: 287).

Moreover, the idea of the social movement is inseparable from that of the conflict. If there are no certain forces that control power and information, there will also be no social movement that struggles against this control, and, therefore, no defense of the subject (Touraine 1995: 163). However, because modernization gave birth to the idea of the subject, Touraine believes that today's notion of subject is different from that of the dawn of the modern era. This is why the social movements of today are different from previous movements, and are referred to as "new social movements."

Touraine's understanding of our contemporary world is based on a planetary vision of the universe being dominated by the two conflicting forces of the globalized markets and national or cultural identities. Therefore, the worlds of technologies and markets, and of cultures, instrumental reason and collective meaning, are being disconnected from one another. This results in the dissociation of the economy, culture, and identities. Touraine calls this dissociation "de-modernization" (Touraine 2000).

One of the most important characteristics of the programmed society is the circulation of cultural meanings within it besides material products. Because of ongoing exposure to new ideas and lifestyles through the media, immigration, and global interdependency, maintaining a coherent sense of self becomes a challenge. By resistance against the domination of neo-liberal forces, the object of conflicts in programmed society becomes the defense of freedom and the ability to give life a special meaning. The "central conflict," i.e. the conflict between the dominated and dominating, therefore, moves in new directions (Touraine 1995).

Being concerned with the cultural critique of the post-industrial society, Touraine argues that:

> No individual, living in the West, at the end of the 20th century, can escape the fear of total loss of meaning, or the fear that private life and the capacity to be a subject are being invaded by propaganda and advertising and by the degradation of the society into a crowd.
>
> (Touraine 1995: 163)

According to Touraine, the subject today is characterized by the attempt to bring together rationality and cultural meanings into a coherent unit. The subject is a process that has developed historically. But, unlike the past, subjectivation is not linked to the nation-state and defense of the rights of the workers or citizens. Instead, it is associated with the individual's life and the challenges that emerge from this contradictory experience (Touraine 2000).

In *Critique of Modernity*, first published in 1992, Touraine gives equal importance to the two concepts of "subjectivation" and "rationalization," as two driving forces of modernity. However, in *Can We Live Together?*, first published in 1997, he tries to reconstruct his previous understanding of "subjectivation" and "rationalization." He claims that, although the given analysis in *Critique of Modernity* is still accurate, the changing character of the nation-state, which has caused de-modernization, has led to transformation of the classical model of rationalization. In the past, before the emergence of the globalized economy, rationalization and ethical individualism could only be contextualized within the concrete framework of the Republican nation-state. Moreover, rationalization could be understood through the conceptualization of human beings as citizens who could actively contribute to the protection of their freedom individually or through a collective act. However, the internationalization of trade and decreasing importance of the nation-state has weakened the notion of the citizen. This has led to a crisis because there is no longer a link between the globalized economy and introverted communities. Therefore, the connection between the productive society (which is a market society today), and self-identity (which is a communitarian identity today), has become distorted. This alteration of the nation-state and self-identity, which goes hand in hand with de-modernization, has led to de-institutionalization. This is why the idea of the subject appears in another context, from that of the early modern era. The subject is now between two worlds—that of instrumentality and that of identity—and its focus is directed toward civil society and culture. Therefore, by acting as a principle for the reconstruction of social experience today, the subject is the only force that can prevent the worlds of instrumentality and of identity from drifting apart. As Touraine puts it; "subject is modernity's sole defender today" (Touraine 2000: 83).

Furthermore, he argues that civil society should construct a set of mediations that are both social and political. These mediations should exist between political programs and social institutions. Civil society cannot function well when social demands are subordinated to a political program. This mediating role is clarified more through the important role given to the defense of the subject in the new social movements. This is meant to free the concept of social movement from political instruments (Touraine 2000).

Political expression of the subject in Touraine's thoughts is democracy. In other words, democracy is the recognition of the other as subject, i.e. as an agent, responsible for a combination of rationality and identity on a personal and collective level. The idea of democracy is primarily identified with that of the society and the subject. This is why Touraine's analysis of the subject in modern society ends with some considerations on democracy (Touraine 1997, 1995). His reflections on democracy are based on some initial arguments. Democracy has been seen a political regime that allows social actors to emerge and act freely. As long as there is a conflict between the ruler and the ruled, the responsibility of individuals towards their common cultural orientations and the pluralism of different kinds is not respected, and the existence of any independent social actor becomes questionable.

As a result, on the one hand, democracy becomes the recognition of subjects, and of the diversity of their attempts for reconciliation of cultural identities (Touraine 1997: 126). On the other hand, this individuation leads to democracy because the individuals will entail the capacity of being subjects. In Touraine's words, "democracy allows individuals to become free subjects who produce their own history, and whose actions can reconcile the universalism of reason, with the particularism of a personal or collective identity" (Touraine 1997: 186).

Touraine (2000: 119–20) concludes that the social movements and democracy are closely linked, and one cannot exist without the other. For Touraine, democracy is both the instrument and the outcome of the institutionalization of social conflicts and, therefore, a prerequisite of social movements. In an undemocratic situation there is the danger that social movements would be distorted by political forces who are aiming to gain access to power apparatuses; or would just be reduced to collective explosions of anger. However, without social movements democracy would be weakened and restricted because the subject would not have enough freedom to act as a social actor.

Historicity is another key concept in Touraine's approach to social movements. As he writes:

> Historicity is the self production of the society through its social conflicts and increasingly with that of the subject, i.e. of the self production of the social actor battling with the logic of consumption. It is through historicity that collective actors, classes and social movements fight for the realization and institutionalization of values.
>
> (Touraine 1996: 317)

As Scott (1996: 79) makes clear, historicity bears the idea of shared norms and values, found in functionalism but, at the same time, its emphasis on struggle and divergence of interests makes it similar to conflict theory. Historicity is an action, exerted by society, on its social and cultural practices through the combination of three components: the model of knowledge, which is the image of society and nature; accumulation, which is linked to society's product; and the cultural model, which is redirected to society's capacity for action upon itself (Touraine 1997: 461). Historicity is a stage of historical development that makes feasible self-reflection on the foundations of social life. However, historicity is not only understood by referring to historical time, but also by referring to the process of social transformation that is the consequence of social action. In other words, historicity is not a certain episode of historical evolution but is the creation of a historical experience. A social movement, therefore, is characterized by the realization of historicity and the self-consciousness of the movement. Social movements aim to gain control over historicity (Touraine 1981, 1995).

Although historicity cannot be separated from class relations, Touraine refuses to define classes within an economic mechanism. Instead, he defines them in reference to how they dispose of knowledge and control information. He intends to illustrate the historicity of society as a cultural field divided by the conflict between two classes: those who dominate the historicity, and those who are being dominated but try to re-appropriate the historicity. Each society, therefore, consists of two main classes: a "ruling class" and a "popular class". The ruling class is in charge of the production of society and its historicity. The popular class, which is dominated by the ruling class, challenges its domination in order to win the historicity for itself. Hence, a society is formed by two opposing movements in Touraine's analysis: one that changes historicity into organizations, order, and power, and another that tries to break down this order and rediscover new orientations and conflicts through "cultural innovation" and "social movements" (Touraine 1981: 31, 60). This explains why the new social movements have replaced the workers' movements as the "central" progressive agency in post-industrial society.

Moreover, he believes that, unlike the workers' movements, today's movements are only interested in liberation of the subject (Touraine 1997: 96). Larger social projects are not their objective. The subject is exposed to the ethical values, which come into conflict with the social order (Touraine 2000: 95). Thus, the functioning of a society is linked to its historicity and its class relations, and, therefore, to its social movements. Subjectivation and social movements fight over the hegemonic meanings of society, i.e. historicity.

Society's capacity for self-transformation defines the level of historicity, and is different for the transition from one level of historicity to another. The state is external with regard to social relations in Touraine's analysis. Because of the systemic character of the society, the transition from one system to another presupposes the existence of a particular agent of historical transformation and a special logic of action, which is external to the society and can only be designated by the state, as an agent that imposes transformation on society. Hence, social movements are concerned with changing life rather than transforming society, and are not forces that transform the present and construct the future. In other words, a social movement emerges into a field of historicity, functions within it, and disappears within the same field (Touraine 1981: 94–95).

New social movements, nomads of the present: Alberto Melucci

Alberto Melucci is an Italian sociologist, and at one point was Touraine's pupil. He has been strongly influenced by Touraine's thoughts. He is one of the founders of the term "new social movement" in sociological literature.

Similar to Touraine, Melucci analyzes social movements within the framework of post-industrial society, or in his own term "complex society." In order to elaborate on the concept of new social movements, he follows the two main assumptions presented by Touraine, i.e. 1) interconnection between modernity and the rise of the subject and 2) structural differences of post-industrial society from industrial society.

According to Melucci (1996c), modernity has offered individuals freedom of action in an open field of possibilities. This means that individuals are less affected by natural constraints, and that technological domination is replacing the traditional power of nature. Furthermore, freedom for the individual has led to acceleration of full realization of his autonomy. Melucci (1996c: 42, 147) claims that the most important legacy of modernity has been the need for and duty of humankind to exist as individuals. This has led human beings to think about themselves as subjects of action, capable of purposive and meaningful behavior. Furthermore, the structure of the complex society, which offers an open space for individuals, provides means and resources for individual identification. Nonetheless, such a space is socially constructed and only can be provided where resources are available. Social construction of such a space does not occur in all kinds of societies; only those societies in which people have at least met their basic material needs. Moreover, individuals should not be linked to the larger body of a family, kingdom, state, party, and class as they were before. This becomes important because being detached from these larger bodies offers the individual enough space for thinking of him-/herself as an individual. Whereas, in the past, social processes affected individuals principally as members of groups and organizations, the achievements of modernity, such as mass culture, rising educational levels, and the generalization of citizenship rights, have made the individual the subject of action. The society acts on the system as a whole, and also on individuals to enable them to define the meaning of their own actions. In such societies individuals have greater access to resources, and this helps them become capable of recognizing the meaning of their actions (Melucci 1996c, 1996a).

Although Melucci does not give a precise explanation about the structure of the "complex society," he believes that at least three main processes have taken place that can help us understand the nature of complex society and its limits (Melucci 1980, 1989, 1996a).

Firstly, information has become the main resource of the complex society. This has contributed to better and easier access to reality. Our everyday life is now embedded in contexts that are increasingly constructed by information and the media. Moreover, as information is internalized by individuals into signs and images, we can say that in complex society the reality is formed by the conscious production and control of information.

Secondly, a planetary system has emerged, which does not leave anything or anybody external to it. In other words, a single unit has appeared in which all problems are globally interdependent. However, the system in which we are living has reached its limits, i.e. there are no borders, no space, and no time beyond it. There is also no other time and no other society exclusive of this system. The categories in which the construction of human experience is grounded have been changed by the "decolonization" of space and "presentification" of time.

The third character of the complex society is that the main actors within the system are individuals who struggle for individuation by participating in, and giving meaning to, various forms of social action. Therefore, the main actors of the complex society are no longer defined by their class consciousness, religious affiliation, or ethnicity.

Another fundamental issue of the complex society in Melucci's thoughts is based on the emergence of new kinds of property. Whereas, in the era of industrial capitalism, property took the form of natural resources, material goods, and capital, in the complex society another kind of property has emerged—humankind's biological and psychological existence. However, Melucci argues that property in its old version has not disappeared from the complex society, but that the new kind of property is becoming more important. Moreover, although, in the past, societies were mainly dependent on energy for their growth, contemporary societies are concerned with the generation of information, control of environment, expansion into space, etc.

Furthermore, Melucci (1989: 55–56) declares the importance of codes, which embody power in the control of information. Through these codes, any antagonistic collective action can broadcast a message to the rest of the society. In other words, collective action becomes a code in itself and its goals are temporary and, to some extent, replaceable. Questioning the implementation of goals, which have been decided by anonymous powers, becomes part of the goals of the movement. In this way these movements question the logic of efficiency and effectiveness.

Melucci (1996a: 99) believes that in societies with high information density, production goes beyond economic relations and it incorporates social relationships, symbols, identities, and individual. Hence, the development and management of complex systems requires increasing intervention in the relational processes and symbolic systems within the social and cultural realm, and it is not simply dependent on controlling the workforce or the transformation of natural resources. Furthermore, although in complex society human beings become subjects of action and capable of purposive behavior, they also function as the coordinates in a network of communality and communication (Melucci 1996c: 42).

Within such a structure, although more people have access to the ownership of the means of production, their ownership still remains under the control of particular groups. Therefore, on the one hand, defense of the identity and predictability of personal existence, and, on the other, access to knowledge, i.e. the type of codes that give shape, size, and meaning to the resources, begin to constitute the substance of the new conflicts. Unlike Habermas (1992), who considers the new movements as reactions to the colonization of the life world, Melucci (1989: 196) believes that the huge investments of time and energy within the movements in order to create groups, centers, communities, and actions, cannot just be defensive. Activities of movements' participants lead to their personal growth and a sense of security against manipulation.

In complex societies, conflicts develop in the crucial areas that produce information and symbolic resources. Thus, the social conflicts move to the cultural sphere, and the first groups to mobilize are those social groups most directly affected by systemic influences on the formation of meaning and who have more access to the resources. The middle class and the newly marginalized groups start growing capacities for developing collective identities, and, therefore, different capacities for developing expectations (Melucci 1989: 54). Through their visible action, these groups aim to announce existing conflicts.

However, their mobilization is limited to a specific time and place, which is different from traditional forms of collective action (Melucci 1989: 55–56).

Moreover, politics functions as mediation between interests, aiming to produce decisions without being the representative of the totality of social life. A level of society exists that stands prior to politics, which delimits and conditions it, and that is the sphere of social relations and interests. But this sphere is mediated through politics. Moreover, there are aspects of human experience related to the inner life of individuals and their interpersonal relationships. These dimensions also remain outside the realm of politics (Melucci 1996a: 212–13).

In his explanation of complex society, Melucci emphasizes the contemporary opportunities for individuation within complex societies. The availability of resources makes it feasible for individuals to reflect on their needs. This reflection helps individuals to develop new cultures of self-expression. In his three-tiered explanation about the reasons an individual joins a social movement, he explains that, firstly, an individual's participation in collective action is due to the encounter of the individual with contradictions of the complex system. Secondly, as has been explained by resource mobilization theory, availability of resources encourages the individual—who is a cost-benefit calculator—to join a collective action. The third level of explanation is related to the psychology of the individual and his/her personal reasons, which, according to Melucci, sometimes go beyond attachments to a certain social group (Melucci 1989: 216).

Production of cultural codes is the main production of a movement, according to Melucci. Interpersonal relationships within the group allow an easy shift from one function to the other. Thus, the energy for public campaigns becomes available through networking, in addition to the individual's self-reflective resources. During the periods that the movement is under pressure and cannot act freely, these networks do not disappear—they reemerge after a while. In the later stages they can even provide the group with new members and new ideas (Melucci 1996a, 1984: 829). The conditions of membership in these networks are personal involvement and solidarity. Multiple memberships and part-time or short-term participation are also possible (Melucci 1984: 829).

In trying to understand the composite character of the new movements, which contain a plurality of levels, with reference to the new structures of the complex society, Melucci (1996c, 1996a) differentiates between the new and old social movements in several aspects: first, the new movements are concerned with the production of information rather than the production or distribution of material goods. Second, participation in the contemporary movements is not directed towards the future. Rather, for the participants of the movement the participation is an end in itself (explaining why Melucci refers to the new social movements as "nomads of the present", see Melucci 1989). Third, in contrast to the previous movements, the private and public lives of the activists are not separated. Instead, in the new movements, there is a correlation between private and public life. This means that there is a link between the production of new meanings and experiences, and the publicly expressed commitments. Living differently and changing society is seen as complementary. The new movements experience the new awareness of living as a member of human species in a totally interdependent human and natural world system. The interrelation between humanity and the wider global universe is one of the important issues raised by these new movements. This interrelation is emphasized by the movements. They are heterogeneous and they are concerned with diverse areas of social life (Melucci 1980, 1996c, 1996a). Above all, the new movements do not believe in the efficiency of the traditional institutions of politics, considering them as inappropriate mediums that do not respond to the new demands of the new society. Thus, contemporary collective action practices forms that are different from the old movements. The most important difference is that they are not concerned with achievements of political goals and they invest a lot of time in constructing forms of organization that are not directed towards gaining political power. Therefore, unlike the proponents of the old movements who were trying to find a way to participate in governance through political parties, the new movements articulate the demands of civil society. Through this, the new movements make the power relations of complex systems more visible. The new movements do not aim to incorporate their claims into the political system but their desire is to propose new values and moral concerns and introduce them into a public culture. It could be said that through the new qualitative needs that have been created by complex society, they expand the boundaries of politics (Melucci and Avritzer 2000: 509). They function as open spaces in which diverse groups and individuals, independent of political organizations, meet and negotiate their social demands. The task of the public space with its different institutions, local committees, etc. is then to publicize their basic problems and demands, and to democratize everyday life. This is how the movements can negotiate the power control (Melucci 1996a).

The movements of the nineteenth century were, at the same time, social actors, class actors, and political actors, and their main aim was to include the working class within the bourgeoisie political system. However, according to Melucci, these two aspects are becoming separated in our present society. On the one hand, there are political actors whose actions are directed towards reform, inclusion, new rights, the opening of the boundaries of the political system, etc. On the other hand, there are actors who are engaged in addressing issues that are purely cultural. However, after the cultural issue is named by social actors, it can later either become a political issue or be addressed through political means (Arvitzer and Lyyra 1997).

The complex society makes rapid institutionalization of the change possible and these new transformations give rise to new social models. As the cultural aspects are increasingly changing, a transformation in mental and relational patterns occurs. Its survival, however, depends on political and institutional forms. Melucci believes that the movements in complex societies operate in the pre-political dimensions of everyday life, but also contain a meta-political aspect. They declare the limits of the politics by recognizing that social processes create demands for politics while occupying spheres prior to or beyond politics. Within their informal networks, the movements create new meanings. But with consciousness raising, they also publicize the basic dilemmas of the complex societies, which cannot be addressed by political means. Therefore, these movements are pre-political and meta-political at the same time. They are pre-political because they are based on everyday life and experiences. They are meta-political because political forces are unable to represent them. In other words, they go beyond the boundaries of politics (Melucci 1989, 1996a).

As influencing the cultural codes is one of the main tasks of the new movements, success or failure are meaningless concepts for them. Movements increase innovation and reinforce reforms. However, redefinition of the meaning of social actions for the whole society is the most important task of a new social movement. This makes them the medium and the message at the same time. According to Melucci, even political success might make the movement weaker because it leads to segmentations and bureaucratization of some groups. Nonetheless, the continuity of the movements depends on the political system because the existence of a social movement will be guaranteed if it finds ways to represent itself in a decision making process (Melucci 1996a, 1984: 830–31).

Therefore, what the movements require is the formation of new intermediate public spheres within civil society, mostly because the expansion and official recognition of public spaces is essential for protecting contemporary movements. The further development of knowledge-producing institutions, fields of collective consumption, media and communications are among the important developments in the field of public sphere. Expansion of public spaces is important for the movements to gain public visibility. However, these public spaces should not be dominated by political parties but they should be neutral entities in which different interests could interact. This kind of public space will make the visibility of the power relations of the complex society more feasible (Melucci 1989).

According to Melucci (1989: 76–77), the changed nature of the new movements influences at least three levels of the society. Firstly, they initiate institutional change through political reforms or the redefinition of organizational practices. Secondly, they select new elites, intellectuals, and activists. Finally, they contribute to innovative cultural practices. However, the most significance of their action is in one fundamental dimension: the movements no longer operate as characters but as signs. This means that, they articulate their action into symbolic challenges that overturn the dominant cultural codes while producing systemic effects in representation of power structures.

Touraine/Melucci model and Iran

As was demonstrated, according to the Touraine/Melucci model, the post-industrial era is a new kind of society, which has structural differences from the industrial society. The newly emerged conflicts and cultural creativities have influenced the way people organize themselves in collective actions. The new movements, therefore, have emerged out of a new social structure, and they have new kinds of social actors and identities, new modes of association and new goals, hence, the social movements of the post-industrial era are "new" to the industrial society.

Modernity and its consequences, especially birth and rebirth of the subject, are Touraine's main focus of social movement analysis, whereas Melucci focuses more on the structural changes of the post-industrial society and its influence on the social movements of the new era.

However, in this model, the process of subjectivation, identity construction, and the birth of the "new society" and "new social movements", has been analyzed with regard to a special (i.e. European) kind of modernity and social system. Dual movements of rationalization and subjectivation, crisis of modernity, the remarkable importance of the market, cultural industries, and significance of information and cultural aspects of the social life in the post-industrial society and the consequent identity crisis, new forms of power and dominations, all consider industrialization, class society, and the nation-state as it appeared in Europe in eighteenth and nineteenth century as their analytical context. This ignores the importance of non-European sociocultural context as well as different dimensions of globalization.

This kind of academic analysis of social structure is bound to the Eurocentric notion of history and transition from feudalism to capitalism, and the European structure of social classes. Ulrich Beck has called this way of looking at society "the container model of society" (Beck 2005), where society is understood as a closed entity with clear social structures and stratifications (as known within the European context). In his book *What is Globalization?*, he suggests that this model should be replaced in the context of globalization (Beck 2005).

Although globalization and interconnectedness of the world have made some aspects of life planetary, which could help us analyze social movements of non-European historical backgrounds according to the Touraine/Melucci model (see the conclusion of Chapter 5), the feasibility of a comprehensive analysis of the social movements in a non-European context within this framework remains questionable.

The Iranians launched the constitutional revolution of 1906, which was the first movement of its kind in the Muslim world. Iran became the first country in the Middle East to nationalize its oil industry. More recently, the revolution of 1979 was one of the most significant revolutions of the twentieth century. The most recent achievement of the Iranian people has been the reform movement, which emerged in the last years of the twentieth century. The movement reached its peak in the uprisings of June 2009 after the election fraud. These massive sociopolitical changes during the last hundred years can definitely not be understood through the framework of a theory that focuses on the Western (European) notion of history and social evolution.

One could say that rationalization and subjectivation (which are direct consequences of modernity according to Touraine/Melucci) are necessary resources for social action and social movements, respectively. This brings the concepts of social action and social movements into a close relationship with modernity. However, modernity and its consequences are not one and the same everywhere. Iran did not go through the same paths of modernity as Europe. That is why the social movements of Iran cannot be analyzed independently from its specific history and structure.

Moreover, the Touraine/Melucci model, like other container models of society, gives us a fixed and static image of social structure. It considers social structure in accordance with the transition from feudalism to capitalism and industrial to post-industrial society. This is bound to the class analysis of the social structure according to the industrialization process, the European model of social class structure and the changes in this structure after the emergence of post-industrial society.

Iran in the latter years of the twentieth century has emerged as a modern nation-state, relatively industrialized, with a highly urbanized and educated population and as a regional power. However, unlike Europe, until the last years of the nineteenth century Iran was still experiencing a traditional state and society. Small communities and tribes were shaping the main social structures of Iran before the twentieth century. Besides, the vast majority of the population was still living in villages and was illiterate. Therefore, Iran at the beginning of the twentieth century was still an unindustrialized society with traditional culture and classes. Moreover, the Iranian state has always remained autocratic and power-centered. This is why the development of democratic institutions in Iran was not as even and profound as in Europe. In 1906, Iranians dedicated themselves to promoting the rule of law and limiting the political authority of the state through the constitutional revolution. Today, after more than a century, Iranians are going to the streets longing for democracy and rule of law. This demonstrates that the dilemma of the state-society relationship has remained unsolved and problematic in Iran. Furthermore, Iran experienced rapid periods of modernization in the twentieth century. The modernization process in most periods was not even and profound. Moreover, unlike Europe, the state has been the main agent of modernization. This has led to the rapid structural changes of the society and culture. Additionally, for many years, foreign powers have been subjecting Iran to different kinds of pressures; leaving Iranians with the historical fears of foreign interference and intervention. Above all, the type of globalization Iran has been experiencing is different from the European version of globalization.[1] Iran has been more exposed to cultural and technological aspects of globalization in comparison with other aspects. However, this does not mean that Iran is not at a crossroads of other global trends. On the political level, for instance, there is the attempt to challenge many of the Iranian laws and practices through international principles. On the economic level, Iran has faced an era of economic liberalization since the late 1980s, which has led to creation of specific unequal structures in the society (Fadaee 2011b). These developmental tendencies have all contributed to the rise of Iranian social movements and their distinctive characteristics, their development, and eventual decline.

Conclusion

An important aspect of any social theory is differentiation of different social structures and contexts. Although the Touraine/Melucci model provides a rich and helpful tool for (new) social movement analysis, similar to many other social theories it adheres to a kind of universalism that neglects the heterogeneity of historical pasts, different developmental paths of the state and society (and their relationship), and various trends of globalization. Obviously, there has been a difference between the processes of modernity, democratization, industrialization, and globalization in Iran and Western Europe. As one of the objectives of this book is to examine the relevance of the Touraine/Melucci model in the Iranian context, the next three chapters will provide an overview of these processes within the framework of the Iranian social movements since the early years of the twentieth century. This offers a basis for further analysis of Touraine/Melucci model in the Iranian context. Chapter 5 links the theoretical assumptions of this chapter to the empirical and historical information of Chapters 2, 3, and 4.

2 Grand social movements of Iran in the twentieth century

Introduction

One objective of this book is to illustrate the development patterns of modern Iranian social movements.[1] Studying these development patterns helps us understand the nature of contemporary movements (such as the environmental movement), as social movements are not isolated entities but a response to current circumstances and, at the same time, result from continuity with the past and historical roots. Moreover, the notability of contemporary movements can only be shown in comparison with previous kinds of collective action. As Tilly (2004) demonstrates, pursuing the historical analysis of social movements helps us to discover general laws of social movement operation and reveals the social processes that propagate different kinds of social movements.

'Organized' collective action in the form of social movement in modern Iran, dates back to about a hundred years ago, when the constitutional movement brought fundamental changes in the political system and social life. In this chapter, my aim is to give an overview of Iranian social movements, from the constitutional revolution of 1905–6, to the reform movement of 1997. My intention is to find out, firstly, whether there was any continuity in social movements during this period. Secondly, I want to investigate the differences of the 1997 reform movement from the previous social movements of modern Iran. An overview of the social structure, the state–society relationship, causes of the movement, the social actors and their identity, the process of mobilization (modes of association), and the achievements of each movement is given briefly. However, my aim is not to provide an in-depth analysis of the periods of social movement uprising, rather to give an overview of Iranian society, and dynamics of the emerged movements during each period.

The constitutional movement[2]

The constitutional movement led to a revolution after which Iran officially entered the modern era, by imposing a constitution and a parliament on the traditional political system of Iran. It started as a response to societal changes during the Qajar dynasty (1781–1925) in the nineteenth century and beginning of the twentieth century. As a consequence of the constitutional revolution, many sections of society were changed. New political and social systems, new institutions, and new forms of expression were introduced.

Iranian society throughout the nineteenth century was an agrarian society, based on small communities and their specific hierarchical social structure and face to face relationships. In most cases, until the end of the nineteenth century, self-sufficient communities were the main component of tribes, villages, and towns. Moreover, less than 20 percent of the population was living in urban areas (Abrahamian 2008). The nature of the government during Qajar was, according to Said Amir Arjomand (1988: 24), patrimonial in Weber's typology. Erwand Abrahamian (2000: 33), however, refers to the structure of the state during Qajar as 'a prototypical oriental despotism' (Abrahamian 2008: 33).

The constitutional movement was a consequence of transformations in Iran since the beginning of the nineteenth century. Nasir al-Din Shah's rein (1848–96), was the most important transformatory period, mainly because of his reformist prime minister, Amir Kabir (1807–52). During his term (1848–51), Amir Kabir implemented different kinds of reforms in mining, agriculture, finance, military, trade, commerce, and education. He was among a group of reformist politicians who favored reforms in the structure of the state and society. According to him, such structural changes would lead Iran towards progress and strength (Amjad 1989: 22). The idea of separating the state from dynastic rule and patrimonial government began to influence Iranian politics at the beginning of the nineteenth century. Incorporation of Iran into the international system of sovereign states in this period led to an understanding of the concept of the state as an organization responsible for the welfare of the whole nation (modern state in contrast to patrimonial state) (Arjomand 1988). Amir Kabir was one of the advocates of the idea of the 'modern state', although no progress was made in changing the patrimonial structures of the state during the nineteenth century. Amir Kabir's most influential achievement was the foundation of the first European style high school (Dar al-Fonun) in Iran in 1851. Modern languages, technical-scientific, and military instructions were taught in this school for the first time by European teachers (see Makki 1982).

Throughout the nineteenth century, Iran became more integrated into the world economy in comparison with its past (Arjomand 1988). Additionally, the introduction of telegraphs, telephones, and post offices facilitated internal and external communications, and accelerated Iran's integration into the world economy (Kasravi 2006; Clawson and Rubin 2006). Nasir al-Din Shah became impressed by European achievements after several trips to Europe, and implemented a series of reforms. Furthermore, he decided to attract foreign trade, resulting in a large number of Europeans coming to Iran, making possible interactions between Europeans and locals (Clawson and Rubin 2006).

By the end of the nineteenth century, these developments made for a different society in Iran from that at the beginning of the century. The first years of the twentieth century witnessed a flourishing of the constitutional movement within the Iranian middle class, which was divided into two different groups at that time as described by Abrahamian (1982). The first group was the "traditional middle class," which operated in the traditional bazaar economy and adhered to traditional Shia ideology. The bazaar functioned as the center of trade, industry, and religious activities, playing an important role in the economic and social life of the people. The bazaars incorporated market places, workshops, and banks. However, because the cities were separated by great distances, and there were always fractions within the organizational and linguistic sectors of the bazaars in each city, different parts of the bazaar always remained separate. Therefore, the traditional middle class only existed as a socioeconomic entity until the last years of nineteenth century, and never became a nationwide political force. But in the late nineteenth century, because of the rapid integration of Iran into the world economy, many urban bazaars faced economic manipulation by Western powers. Economic integration led to an ever-increasing dependence of the Iranian traders on the world market, making it difficult to develop domestic industries (Keddie 1981: 63). Furthermore, increased international trade, introduction of the telegraph and post systems, and of newspapers, and the improvement of old roads, started to shape the political awakening of civil society and class consciousness of the traditional middle class (Abrahamian 1982; Arjomand 1988).

The second group of the middle class was known as the "intelligentsia," which was the new and professional middle class (Abrahamian 1982). They advocated the philosophy of the Enlightenment and therefore, of a parliamentary democracy (Arjomand 1988). Being influenced by Europe and European philosophy, they had a different worldview from that of the traditional middle class. As Abrahamian (1982: 50–51) has explained:

> They espoused not the divine right of the kings, but the inalienable rights of man. They promulgated not the advantages of royal despotism and political conservatism, but the principles of liberalism, nationalism, and even socialism. They venerated not the shadow of God on Earth, but the triumvirate of equality, liberty, and fraternity. Moreover, they not only introduced into the vocabulary of contemporary Iran numerous Western words, such as despot, feudal, parliament, social, democrat, and aristocrat, but also injected modern meanings into many old words. For example, *estebdad* changes in meaning from 'monarchy' to 'despotic monarchy'; *mellat* from 'religious community' to secular 'nationality'; and *mardom* from the 'people' without any political connotations to 'the people' with its democratic and patriotic connotations.
>
> (Abrahamian 1982: 50–51)

Several factors led to preparation of society for the constitutional movement during this period. Firstly, the intelligentsia was anxious for change. Secondly, the traditional middle class was left defenseless against foreign competitors. Thirdly, the second half of the nineteenth century led to a dramatic decline in living standards due to Western competition and decline of the gross national product. Moreover, many concessions and privileges were given to foreigners, compared with the first half of the century. Above all, the tyranny of the Qajars remained unchanged. The combination of all these factors gradually generated support among the Iranian people for the constitutional movement (see Abrahamian 1982; Keddie 2006).

Although prior to 1890 most of the intelligentsia was hostile to ulama (the religious leaders), from then onwards the intelligentsia and ulama began collaborating. This collaboration was rooted in the fact that some ulama became effective opponents of the regime's policy towards selling Iran's resources to foreigners. Besides, because of the influence of ulama among the people, the intelligentsia could count on their mobilizing force (Keddie 2006: 59).

The tobacco movement of 1891–2 was the first alliance of the intelligentsia and the traditional middle class, before the constitutional revolution. In return for a personal gift of 25,000 pounds to Nasir al-Din Shah, an annual rent of 15,000 pounds to the state, and 25 percent share of the profits for Iran, an Englishman, Major Talbot, was given a

50-year monopoly over the distribution and exportation of tobacco, which was based on small-scale production of family farms. Although this was not publicly announced at the time, the fact that foreigners could influence the tobacco the people were planting made them worried. In addition, as tobacco was widely used in Iran, so the threat of this monopoly was felt nationwide by all groups and classes. The first move started from the bazaar. The bazaar in Shiraz, the main tobacco-growing region, was shut down because of the arrival of company agents. This shutdown quickly spread to other big cities (Kasravi 2006; Abrahamian 1982). At the same time, the intelligentsia organized secret societies (known as *anjomans*) and started mobilizing the masses. This was mostly done through different kinds of issued papers and public placards condemning the concession. Furthermore, the intelligentsia directly wrote to movement officials protesting against the concession (Poulson 2006: 91–2).

A general *fatwa* (a religious opinion issued by an Islamic scholar) by a religious leader against the use of any tobacco, led to a nationwide boycott of tobacco and all the tobacco shops were closed. This led to a crisis. The boycott ended after 6 months of actions, massive protests, and demonstrations, which led to the nullification of the concession. This was the first successful mass protest in modern Iran in which ulama, modernists, merchants, and ordinary people brought about a change in the regime's policies through a collective movement (Keddie 2006: 62; Elton 2001: 116).

In the years after the tobacco movement public debt increased rapidly, and there was a breakdown of law in the provinces. Even though Nasir al-Din Shah introduced a number of reforms during the earlier period of his reign, in his last years, after the tobacco movement, he lost interest in his reforms and intensified political repression (Elton 2001: 118). Few concessions were sold, expansion of Dar al-Fonun was not allowed, the opening of new schools became illegal, publications faced strict censorship, and government scholarships for study abroad decreased (Abrahamian 1982: 73–74).

After Nasir al-Din Shah died, power passed to his son, Mozaffar al-Din Shah (1896–1906), who was not a strong ruler. He followed his father's unpopular economic policies but this was combined with a mildness in police control. This liberal political atmosphere allowed for the reemergence of some newspapers, and many organized groups and associations (Kasravi 2006). Rather than what Mozzafar al-Din Shah had hoped for, his liberal policies did not satisfy the opposition and the discontent with the government encouraged the opposition to form semi-secret organizations in Tehran and other cities (Keddie 2006: 65).

In *Iran between Two Revolutions*, Abrahamian (1982: 76–8) describes the nature of the five most important organizations that emerged at that time. Two were influenced by the revolutionary socialism of Russian Marxism (the Secret Center and the Social Democratic Party); one reflected the radical positivism of Saint-Simon and the liberal humanism of August Comte (the Society of Humanity); and one was a reflection of the ideological homogeneity and sociological diversity of the early intelligentsia (the Revolutionary Committee). Unlike these four, the fifth organization was organized by, and replicated the ideology of, the traditional middle class (the Secret Center). This organization established contact with two of the important *mojtaheds*, i.e. Behbahani and Tabatabai in Tehran.

Historically, ulama and the traditional class were bound together. Ulama and bazaaris were from the same families. Bazaaris were paying levies, which were the main source of the ulama's income. At the same time, ulamas were providers of the religious ceremonies for the bazaar. Moreover, faithfulness and religious observance were important aspects of bazaaris. Being aware of the religious beliefs of people, the traditional middle class knew that collaborating with two of the most important ulamas would encourage the masses to participate in revolutionary politics (Keddie 2006: 30).

As a result of the activities of the mentioned organizations and groups, three different groups played a central role in the constitutional movement (Abrahamian 1982): the first was the intelligentsia, providing the ideological base for the movement. The ulamas were the second who, due to their influence among the masses, had the potential of mobilizing the people. The third group was the bazaaris who, as the center of economic activities of the country, could paralyze the bazaar through strikes and protests. This threatened the government as the bazaar was one of the most important institutions of the society.

In their first phase, the unrests were mainly protest movements that reflected economic issues. But throughout 1904–5, a coalition emerged that had other demands. Three important facts directed the economically oriented protests of the early twentieth century towards a revolutionary movement for a parliament and a constitution. Firstly, the semi-secret organizations played an important role in consciousness raising. Secondly, the traditional middle class and the intelligentsia collaborated with each other. This collaboration brought a huge number of people together, despite different ideologies. Finally, the Russo-Japanese war of 1904 and the Russian revolution of 1905 reinforced the revolutionary sentiment among Iranians. In addition, Iranians observed

Russians facing economic problems and a dictatorship established a parliament (Clawson and Rubin 2006: 42).

Although by 1905 society was ready for the constitutional movement, the economic crisis of early 1905 provided the final push. A bad harvest throughout the country, a sudden disruption of northern trade caused by the Russo–Japanese war, and the revolution in Russia, all led to an economic crisis that generated public protests (Abrahamian 1982: 81).

The first protest was a peaceful procession during the religious mourning of Muharram. Shopkeepers and moneylenders were the main participants of this protest. They demanded the dismissal of the Naus, a Belgian customs administrator. The second protest was in December 1905, when the governor of Tehran punished several merchants for not lowering their sugar prices as was ordered by the government. As the punished merchants were respected people of the bazaar, i.e. the traditional middle class, the bazaaris and ulama challenged the leadership by closing the stores and seeking sanctuary. Four main demands were sent to the government: replacement of the governor, dismissal of Naus, enforcement of the *sharia* (body of Islamic religious law), and establishment of the House of Justice. The third protest occurred in summer 1906, because of the failure of the Shah to establish a House of Justice and dismiss Naus, and because of the police arrest of a local preacher, who was denouncing the government in public. The third protest became a mass protest of members of many secret organizations, students, bazaaris, and other people, who joined the big crowd. Although the government reacted violently to the protest, with the leadership of Tabatabai and Behbahani, further large-scale demonstrations were organized. Moreover, in the holy city of Qom, the ulamas went on strike.

After a few days, a group of merchants and theology students went to the British embassy to seek refuge there. In *Political Economy of Modern Iran*, Katouzian explains that the British embassy granted the people refugee status because this would give them diplomatic advantages against Russia. In addition, they could introduce themselves as proponents of democracy and freedom (see Katouzian 1981: 59). The next day, others joined them. After a few days, the number of refugees passed 13,000 and the bazaars were closed (Kasravi 2006: 137–8). At the same time, members of the secret organizations were openly trying to raise the protestors' knowledge of the political issues (Elton 2001: 121).

The crowd was drawn mostly from the bazaars, organized by a committee of the members of the secret organizations, who were also organizing women's demonstrations outside the embassy's garden where the demonstrators were gathered. According to Nazim al-Islam Kermani, after 1 week the political science and agriculture students of Dar al-Fonun made the embassy "one vast open air school of political science" (Abrahamian 1982: 84). The most interesting event was that the crown prince Mohammad Ali Mirza joined the activists in Tabriz. He expressed his support for the activists in a telegram to his father. After this, many telegrams from other cities were sent to the Shah in support of the activists (Kasravi 2006: 138). As a result, the refugees' demands expanded from some primary needs, and after a few days people began calling for a constitution and a parliament. It is important to mention that during these late stages of the movement, in addition to the intelligentsia, the ulama and religious community, almost all of the merchants, shopkeepers and artisans, many of the landlords, and most of the ordinary urban public supported, and participated in, the revolution (Katouzian 2003: 27).

The Shah accepted the people's demands. The first parliament was opened in October 1906, and the fundamental constitution was prepared. Mozaffar al-Din Shah signed Iran's first constitution in December 1906.

The revolution was later followed by a civil war and Mohammad Ali Shah (Mozaffar al-Din's son) bombed the parliament. The revolution did not lead to the establishment of a centralized, modern state (Arjomand 1988: 59); however, the constitution remained an important heritage after the revolution. In addition to the constitution, a series of financial reforms were implemented and, later, the parliament began to control foreign interventions (Keddie 1981: 71).

The national oil movement

From the constitutional revolution until 1920, Abrahamian (2008: 62) argues that "Iran was a classic failed state." By this, he means that the government was not centralized and the ministries were not influential outside the capital. Some provinces were ruled by warlords and others by armed rebels. In general, people were desperate to find a hero to rescue them from this chaotic situation (Abrahamian 2008: 62).

During Reza Shah's reign (1925–41), Iran became more centralized. This was possible through implementation of a series of modernization programs, such as modernizing the army and raising the state revenues through taxation, banking, and customs reform, road construction, and the Trans-Iranian railway. Civil bureaucracy was expanded and the judicial system was secularized under Reza Shah, and European-style education was introduced. Also, the participation of women in education, the economy, and public life was accelerated (Arjomand 1988; Cronin 2003).

However, despite the mentioned changes, compared with the years after the constitutional movement, there was a decline in independent activities and institutions. The press was state-run and newspapers were either censored or shut down. Moreover, under Reza Shah all the social and political institutions that could have played an important role in the development of the civil society were banned, such as political parties, associations, etc. The intelligentsia was pushed out of the political realm, and Great Britain was strongly involved in the national affairs of Iran while benefiting from the trade in natural resources (Ghani 1999). At the same time, during the Second World War, Iran was divided by the Soviets in the north, and the British in the south. The occupation and the newly emerged economic and social problems as a result of the war, made the economic situation of the country problematic. Therefore, dissatisfaction with the government grew. Moreover, although Reza Shah introduced law, discipline, and facilities such as schools, trains, buses, radios, cinemas, telephone, etc., his modernization programs went hand in hand with repression and corruption (Abrahamian 2008: 91).

In 1942, Reza Shah was succeeded by his son Mohammad Reza. In contrast with Reza Shah, Mohammad Reza Shah followed a more liberal political attitude. Many political prisoners were released and, as a result, from the beginning of the 1940s, oppositional organizations, protests, and trade unions started to emerge. Even the 27 younger members of the famous "53" Marxists imprisoned in 1937 by Reza Shah, announced the formation of a political organization called Hezb-e Tudeh-ye Iran (The Party of the Iranian Masses), which later played an important role in the national oil movement and 1979 revolution. In addition, the atmosphere of a relatively free press led to the emergence of many newspapers that promoted political and social change. Twenty-two major parties were active between 1941 and 1946, although Tudeh was the only one that developed coherent structures. Moreover, there were many associate parties in provincial centers and many student groups had emerged. Every political group had at least one newspaper as a result of press activity. By 1951, at the dawn of the oil nationalization, in Tehran alone about 700 papers were in print (Ansari 2003: 78–9). As a consequences of these civil liberties, the cities were experiencing a politically organized urban population (Keddie 2006: 1981).

Moreover, although society was socially and politically polarized after the war, Iran was facing many social and economic problems.

Conflicts and foreign interference increased. Wartime and post-war inflation made life difficult for most social groups, and put them under different kinds of pressure. Furthermore, because of the increased demand for urban goods and services, increasing urbanization, development of communication infrastructure, educational reforms, etc., and the consequent emergence of new urban social groups, cities became the sites of unrest and social mobilization (Keddie 1981: 128).

Three main social groups were at the center of social changes and mobilizations during this period. Accumulation of capital by Iranians, who profited from the war, led to creation of a new middle class. This group supported reforms to improve economic stability and governmental efficiency. Additionally, they demanded limitation of the power of foreign capital. Another growing social group at this time was the intelligentsia. Because of unemployment and the economic problems in society, this group was active in many social protest movements of the time, demanding fundamental reforms. The lower middle class was the third social group, and was at the center of the post-war social dissatisfactions. This group profited from wartime demands, but later suffered from the post-war economic crisis. Although the lower middle class was not a new social group, the post-war economic crisis changed its position, which was threatened by the competition of foreign goods and services and by the government's favoring of the new middle class and upper classes. Moreover, it was threatened by reduction of Iranians' purchasing power due to further integration into the world economy (Keddie 1981: 128).

A 7-year development plan was implemented by the Americans to reduce the post-war crisis. However, the failure of the plan, and resultant problems and dissatisfactions, led to the emergence of a social movement with the goal of nationalizing the oil industry (Keddie 1981).

Apart from the economic crisis and the consequent dissatisfaction generated, the Iranians had been suffering at the hands of the Anglo–Iranian Oil Company (AIOC) and its unjust policies for a long time. In order to analyze the national oil movement, one should first consider that the Iranian oil industry had been controlled by the British through the AIOC since its establishment in 1909. From the very beginning Iranians had many grievances against the AIOC, mostly related to the small amount of revenue that Iran received from the company. Moreover workers and their families were living in deplorable conditions (Kinzer 2003: 67). After the war these discontents grew and people began to see the AIOC as the major cause and as a channel for British influence and control over Iran (see Keddie 1981). In order to prevent further dissatisfaction, the British reached an accord with the AIOC known as the Gass-Gulshaiyan supplement agreement. Its main concession was to increase royalties to Iran. An informal *majlis* (Iranian parliament) opposition started a campaign against the new supplement as the fifteenth majlis was about to conclude, the group continued its opposition until the end of the fifteenth majlis (Makki 1991). As Mohammad Mosaddegh wrote in his memoirs:

> In the fifteenth majlis of which I was not a deputy, some deputies gave explanations, and enlightened public opinion about the harms of the 1933 Agreement, and it was on the basis of such a public awareness of the issue that the oil industry was nationalized through the country.
>
> (Mussadeq 1988: 376)

With the closure of the fifteenth majlis, the Shah and his proponents decided to rig the elections of the sixteenth majlis and obtain the majority. In October 1949, under the leadership of Mosaddegh, a crowd of politicians, university students, and bazaar traders gathered in the palace grounds to protest against the absence of free elections and negotiate with the court minister (Abrahamian 1982: 252).

In *Iran Between Two Revolutions*, Abrahamian (1982: 252) explained the combination of this representative committee. He states that this committee contained three groups. The first group included some prominent anti-court politicians, the second some politicians connected to the bazaar, and the third, and most important, comprised a number of young, Western-educated radicals from the intelligentsia. The consequent unrests caused by the demonstration forced the court to promise to end electoral irregularities. In addition, the representative committee considering Mosaddegh who played the role of their leader formed a broad coalition, which was named the National Front (in Persian known as *Jebhe-ye Melli*). However, the National Front, in its first public declaration, did not raise the oil issue. Rather they were concerned with the election issue and had three specific demands: honest elections, lifting of martial law, and freedom of the press. Five organizations (The Iran Party, The Toiler's Party, The National Party of Iran and the Society of Muslim Warriors and Devotees of Islam) subsequently joined the National Front's main body. Mosaddegh became their serving leader (Abrahamian 1982).

The Iran Party had been set up by a number of young Iranian technocrats who had liberal and social democratic ideologies. They were opposed to dictatorship, foreign domination, and bureaucratic corruption, and were sympathetic towards the Soviet Union and the Tudeh Communist Party. The class base of the Iran Party was derived from the professional middle class, especially engineers and lawyers. Many of its members were technocrats and academics. They also had influence among modern educated women and among university students, and a women's organization and a youth organization were formed. They called for strengthening the constitutional monarchy (i.e. transforming the Shah into a ceremonial state), establishing national independence, and overthrowing the landed aristocracy. They used newspapers as their medium of communication and were among the few groups who remained loyal to Mosaddegh until the end of his premiership (Abrahamian 1982; Katouzian 1990).

The Toiler's Party was a coalition between Baqai, a former democrat and an activist for free elections, and Khalil Maleki, a Marxist intellectual, who had left the Tudeh Party. Their main programs were to establish a genuine constitutional monarchy, eliminate upper class privileges, encourage small industries, and national independence. They became famous among workers and students, attracting them in large numbers. Although they had socialist ideas, in the first public announcement of the party, they pledged support not only to Mosaddegh, but also to Kashani and Makki, the two favorites of the bazaar. The party had two papers, one was just directed towards the bazaar whereas the other was more of an intellectual paper, which propagated socialism and constitutionalism. Later, Khalil Maleki accused Baqai of collaborating with anti-patriotic elements, and formed a new organization called Niru-ye Sevvom (Third Force), which remained an ardent supporter of Mosaddegh (see Behrooz 2000; Zabih 1966; Katouzian 1990).

The National Party was founded by a young law student, Dariush Foruhar. The party was a detached wing of the popular nationalist movement, which was founded during the Second World War. They were anti-communist, anti-capitalist, anti-Semitic, and anti-clerical. Their main proposal was to rebuild Iran. They drew most of their members from high school students in Tehran, but were not an important part of the National Front (Katouzian 1990; Abrahamian 1982).

The Society of Muslim Warriors, and, closely associated with them, a small organization known as the *Fadaiyan-e Eslam* (Devotees of Islam), were two religious organizations supporting the national oil movement. Kashani was the leader of the Society of Muslim Warriors, who later became the religious leader of the national oil movement.

The bazaaris, seminary students, small shopkeepers, and, in general, the traditional middle class were the main supporters of the organization. They mostly called for the implementation of the sharia, repeal of Reza Shah's secular laws, re-imposition of the veil (Reza Shah banned women from wearing veils in public), protection of national industries, and Muslim unity against the West. Unlike the Society of Muslim Warriors, Fadaiyan-e Eslam was radical and fundamentalist. Their program went beyond the general sharia beliefs of the Society of Muslim Warriors. They emphasized dogmatic aspects of Islam and demanded the implementation of specific rules, such as the prohibition of alcohol, tobacco, opium, films, and gambling; cutting off of the hands of criminals; a ban on all foreign clothes; and the veiling of women, in order to re-impose traditional roles. Their membership was drawn from the youth employed in the lower sections of Tehran bazaar. Although their methods and beliefs were different from those of the bazaaris, they helped Kashani (the leader of the bazaaris) organize bazaar strikes and demonstrations. Both groups were actively involved in the movement and helped rally the public in support of the nationalization of oil. Both Kashani and the Fadaiyan-e Eslam subsequently turned against Mosaddegh, claiming that he ignored sharia in his government (Katouzian 1990; Abrahamian 1982).

Mosaddegh, the leader of the movement, was educated in Europe, and entered politics shortly after the constitutional revolution. He served in various political positions (parliament deputy, governor of the Fars province, finance minister, foreign minister, governor of Azerbaijan province, and twice as the prime minister). In the first period of his political activity, before becoming the leader of the national oil movement, he became famous for his opposition to the trans-Iranian railway project, re-organization of the courts and the Justice Department, and for forbidding women from wearing veils. He was elected as Tehran's first deputy to the fourteenth majlis in 1943 (Abrahamian 1982).

Thus, the National Front represented two different forces: the traditional middle class (the bazaaris) and the modern middle class (the intelligentsia). The first group believed in Islam as a way of life and in ulama as the guardians of the Shia community. Their followers were inspired by traditional schools and preaching, and were tied to the bazaar traders and contested state intervention in the market economy. The second group was mostly supported by graduates of secular state schools. Religion was considered to be a private matter, and it was believed that the Western-educated intelligentsia could organize society most effectively. In sum, the traditional middle class was conservative, religious, theocratic, and market-oriented, whereas the intelligentsia was modern, secular, technocratic, and socialist (Abrahamian 1982: 259–60).

Apart from the mentioned organizations that became part of the national oil movement, the role of the Communist Party of Tudeh, as the major political party at that time, should also be analyzed. *Hezb-e Tudeh-ye Iran* (Party of the Masses of Iran) was an Iranian Communist Party established in 1941 after the abdication of Reza Shah. The founders of the party were university-educated intellectuals who had reached Marxism through the left-wing movements of Western Europe. The members were mostly intellectuals, workers, artisans, and craftsmen. Soon after formation, they announced a program, established branches in many big cities, organized meetings and conferences, and had their own newspapers. It was the Tudeh Party that introduced the concept of "class consciousness" into the Iranian political discourse (Zabih 1966). In 1949, Tudeh was banned because of a failed assassination attempt against Mohammad Reza Shah. But an improvement in the political situation meant that the Tudeh re-started its activity by publishing a newspaper and establishing organizations, especially for women and youth. Therefore, in 1951, when the national oil movement was in its most important period, Tudeh was playing a major political role. Being an experienced party based in urban areas and skilled in underground activities, it performed a key role in major trade union organization, by unionizing 75 percent of the industrial labor force. Additionally, it had the support of many intellectuals (Behrooz 2000: 5).

Tudeh was one of the leading forces in the national oil movement up to the events of March 1951. It contributed to the movement mainly by organizing strikes in oil fields and holding rallies in different cities in May 1951. Further, it mobilized many mass demonstrations in favor of the National Front. Although in the beginning Tudeh supported Mosaddegh and the National Front, it subsequently faced a crisis in leadership policies. One group of leaders was willing to support Mosaddegh. They believed that the National Front's opposition to the British oil company and their plan to redistribute land was important in undermining the feudal class structure. In contrast, another group opposed the National Front, calling Mosaddegh the leader of the national bourgeoisie. They charged that he was aligned with American imperialism, whose plan was to expel the British and its oil industry from Iran in order to replace this with American firms. The latter group was successful in winning the debate, and started a series of actions against Mosaddegh (Behrooz 2000; Abrahamian 1982; Musaddeq 1988).

In the sixteenth majlis, a coalition of some of the National Front's leaders was elected. Mosaddegh was among them. In November 1950, the Majlis' Oil Committee, headed by Mosaddegh, recommended rejection of the Oil Supplemental Agreement. However, the new prime minister, Razmara, disagreed. Razmara was assassinated on 7 March 1951, by a member of the Fadaiyan-e Eslam. Following his assassination, the majlis easily passed a bill for nationalization of Iranian oil in March 1951. The AIOC was nationalized and Mosaddegh, as the champion of oil nationalization, was elected prime minister. In 1952, the Shah tried to replace Mosaddegh but this sparked riots nationwide and Mosaddegh came back to power with even greater support. However, in aftermath of March 1951, the country faced economic crisis and foreign countries refused to buy Iranian oil. Consequently, the Abadan refinery, which was one of the largest world's refineries, was closed.

During the two periods of his tenure, Mosaddegh followed through with the nationalization of the oil industry in spite of many threats and problems caused by the British and Americans. Furthermore, under Mosaddegh's government, political parties and groups were free and the government was tolerant towards various interests. The ministers were accountable to the majlis and the public. The courts were independent, and all the military and other special courts were abolished. Thus, we can conclude that the movement had two main outcomes: firstly, a democratic government was established, and, secondly, the desire of Iranians for national sovereignty was pursued (Gasiorowski 2005).

In August 1953, a military coup d'état, which was supported by the British and the American CIA, was successful in overthrowing Mosaddegh's government. He was imprisoned for 3 years, and lived under house arrest for the rest of his life.

After the coup the oil crisis was resolved and Iranian oil started flowing again. The AIOC tried to resume production, but in opposition to public opinion they failed to do so. Instead, the National Iranian Oil Company, an international consortium, was established and the AIOC was only one of its members. Although the British and Americans remained influential in Iranian politics in the years after the coup, and many problems remained unresolved, such as the result of the oil nationalization movement, after many years of British control, Iran's oil industry became nationalized.

The revolutionary movement of 1979

Almost 30 years after the national oil movement, the Shah of Iran was facing different challenges from different segments of the population.

These challenges finally led to the transformation of the political system from monarchy to a republic. The post-Mosaddegh years saw a notable change in the sociopolitical situation in Iran. The USA, whose influence in the post-war period was limited, started to become the dominant foreign power in Iran. The rising influence of the USA was evident in the increased percentage of its share in oil taken, the Iranian military's increasing dependence on American military hardware and advisors, the role of American advisors in civilian and governmental programs, and in diverse forms of investment (Keddie 2006: 132).

After 1953, Mohammad Reza Shah restarted the expansion of three components of his state: the military, the bureaucracy, and the court patronage system (Abrahamian 2008: 123). Although the oil industry remained formally nationalized, it was under the control of an international association of oil companies. Furthermore, the oil revenues of the state increased dramatically and provided the Shah and his government with a lot of capital. Much of this capital and foreign aid were used for military purposes (Kaefler 1988: 167). Moreover, the coup against Mosaddegh was followed by the consolidation of power. The Shah developed a dictatorial regime after 1953, which was increasingly repressive towards opponents. He banned all oppositional political parties and many of the activists of the national oil movement were arrested or fled the country. In 1957, the Shah decided to have an effective internal security service and set up the large organization SAVAK, which was supported by the American CIA and Israeli Mossad. From then until 1975, only two political parties were allowed to operate. One was the "government" *Melliyun* Party, and the other was the "opposition" *Mardom* Party. Each proposed candidates for the majlis, but these parties were not allowed to suggest any candidates not approved by SAVAK. Therefore, the system was not really a two-party system. The majlis was powerless, and the prime minister was an appointee of the Shah. In fact, these two political parties were both wholly under the Shah's domination (Abrahamian 1982: 425–26).

By 1975, however, the Shah established a single party, obliging all Iranians to join. "The degree of state control had gone far beyond the other repressive regimes in third world countries," Fred Halliday (1979: 50).

As explained by Looney (1982: 3–5) and Katouzian (1981), Iran's economic situation before the overthrow of the Shah within the period of 1965–77 was a period of rapid industrialization and modernization centered in Tehran. This rapid industrialization and modernization generated discontent in the mid-1970s within the displaced and economically weakened sections of society. Moreover, due to major demographic shifts and migration to cities, the country was urbanizing rapidly, leading to a dramatic decline in the agricultural workforce and the increasing importance of industrial wage labor in the Iranian economy. The regime did not succeed in controlling inflation, and military expenditures accelerated remarkably after 1973. Furthermore, the bazaar merchants' dependence on state credits to finance many of their activities threatened their economic role in society.

However, the positive results of the economic policies of Shah should not be ignored: the rate of industrial growth was one of the highest in the world (per capita GNP rising from about $200 to $1,000 from 1963 until the late 1970s), and the share of manufacturing in the GNP rose from 11 to 17 percent. This change in manufacturing resulted in the rapid growth of some leading industries (Keddie 1981; Abrahamian 1982). Moreover, money was spent on human resources. The number of hospitals and health clinics increased and the educational system was dramatically improved—the number of kindergartens, elementary schools, secondary schools and technical, vocational and teacher training schools increased. In addition, the number of students registered at foreign universities increased, especially in North America and Western Europe. Furthermore, the government built some new campuses in different cities, which improved the college enrollment rate in Iran. As a result, between 1963 and 1977 the educational system grew more than threefold (Abrahamian 1982: 431).

As the new changes were mostly in towns, this had a great influence on the growth of the urban population. Between 1956 and 1976, the urban population grew from 31 percent to 47 percent of the total population, as a result of migration from rural areas (Arjomand 1988: 74). The state's neglect of the agricultural sector contributed to the discontent in urban and rural areas. Moreover, the government had failed to address social equality (Daneshvar 1996: 63). In general, fast economic growth and rapid industrialization led to an improvement in human resources and growth in the urban population, but also an increase in inequality among different sections of the society. The increased inequality engendered discontent among different segments. At the same time, the bazaar merchants felt that their economic position in society was threatened (Daneshvar 1996).

Improvement in the educational sector within the decade of 1966–76 was striking. The number of people with higher education degrees increased four times and enrolment in higher education increased threefold (Arjomand 1988: 74). The revolutionary ideas of the middle classes were mostly a consequence of this enormous development in education during these years (Arjomand 1988, Abrahamian 1982).

At the same time, state policies favored capital-intensive foreign firms over small-scale domestic producers. Most importantly, US aid and technical assistance provided the opportunity for American firms and personnel to become involved in many large-scale projects inside Iran. These increased imports of food, capital goods, and many consumer goods. As a result, the country experienced rapid inflation. Furthermore, the income gap grew in the 1960s and 1970s. This became particularly striking after 1974, when oil income decreased after the great price rise (Keddie 1981: 170–74; Daneshvar 1996: 46). As Halliday (1979: 298) explains, thousands of people who demonstrated in Tehran and other big cities in the later phase of revolution were members of the urban poor who had experienced the negative aspects of the oil boom, i.e. food shortage and inflation.

By the mid-1970s, Iran was experiencing three separate phenomena: rapid modernization, political repression, and a change in the social structure of society (Abrahamian 1982). These changes intensified social tensions and unrest in three major ways. Firstly, the combined size of the intelligentsia and the urban working class was growing fast, and these groups posed the most direct challenge to the state. Further, the dissatisfaction of the intelligentsia and urban working class was increasing because they did not have any representative organizations (e.g. professional associations, trade unions, independent newspapers, and political parties). Secondly, the regime's method of development widened the gap between the haves and have-nots. In the 1970s, according to the International Labor Office, Iran had one of the worst unequal income distributions of the world. Finally, the White Revolution—a program of reform implemented by the Shah—and the subsequent oil boom led to a drastic rise in public expectations. However, the state did not respond to these expectations effectively. Iran still had some of the worst infant mortality and doctor–patient rates in the Middle East. It also had one of the lowest percentages of the population in higher education, 68 percent of adults remained illiterate, 60 percent of children did not complete primary school, and only 30 percent of applicants could enter universities (Abrahamian 2008).

Within different segments of society, religious and secular (leftists and liberals) forces were important in formation of opposition to the Shah. Additionally, in the late stages of the revolution, i.e. by autumn 1978, large numbers of industrial workers, and white collar employees had also joined the opposition (see Parsa 1989; Abrahamian 1982).

According to Daneshvar (1996) and Halliday (1979), in the beginning the movement was supported by students and intellectuals, or in other words the educated classes, who were demanding political freedom and democracy. But this movement gradually made the mullahs and other segments of the society conscious of their position as well. Moreover, Ayatollah Khomeini's promises of democracy and progress went hand in hand with his uncompromising opposition against the regime, and his interpretation of Islam as essentially against monarchy persuaded the revolutionaries to support him (Daneshvar 1996: 194; Halliday 1979; Kaefler 1988: 178).

Khomeini (1902–89), who served as the political leader of the 1979 Iranian Revolution, was *Marja-e Taqlid* (source to imitate and follow) to many Shia Muslims and a lecturer in Najaf and Qom seminaries before entering politics. He was a teacher of political philosophy, Islamic history, and ethics, and he authored many books and articles on these subjects. Khomeini became the leader of Shia Muslims in 1961 after the death of Ayatollah Borujerdi. His first official opposition to the Shah was in 1962 when the Shah decided to abolish the requirements of being male and Muslim for election to local assemblies. Khomeini's second official opposition was in 1963, when Shah announced the White Revolution. The White Revolution was a program of reform, calling for land reform, nationalization of forests, sale of state-owned enterprises to private interests, electoral changes to enfranchise women and allow non-Muslims to hold office, profit-sharing in industry, and a literacy campaign in the nation's schools. Khomeini boycotted the referendum on the White Revolution and many religious leaders followed suit. The boycott brought the Shah and the clerics into opposition. In 1964, Khomeini denounced the Shah because of the diplomatic immunity he granted to American military personnel in Iran. Following his opposition to the mentioned law, Khomeini was arrested and sent to exile in Iraq, Turkey, and finally France. His opposition to the Shah and being sent to exile, made him popular among different segments of the society. In early 1970, Khomeini gave a series of lectures in Najaf on Islamic government. He demanded freedom and social justice. Whereas other oppositional groups were repressed, Khomeini was able to issue political statements through his supporters and while he was in France he had extensive access to international media. In the late 1970s he became the most influential leader of the revolution and led it to its final stage (Khomeini and Algar 1981; Martin 2003).

Because of their religious basis of Shia thoughts and their coalition with ulama, the bazaaris stand against westernization made them important forces not only in the constitutional and national oil movements, but also they provided support for the revolutionary movement of 1979 (Abrahamian 1982).

In addition to the bazaar forces and ulamas who influenced traditional Islamic forces, two other groups the "Freedom Movement" and "Islamic Mujahidin," were important among Muslim intellectuals. Both these groups were Muslim, but they held more modern beliefs than the traditional bazaaris.

The Freedom Movement was established in the 1960s, during the political liberalization and partial relaxation of repression in the early 1960s. The leadership of this group included some supporters of Mosaddegh. The organization was fully revived in 1977, and played a role in the political mobilization of that period. Because of their Islamic beliefs, they had some ties to the mosques, and because they mostly belonged to the upper middle class, they had the support of some of the professional and white collar employees (see, e.g. Abrahamian 1982).

The Islamic Mujahidin split from the Freedom Movement in 1965, and their ideology was a mixture of Marxist philosophy and Islamic philosophy. Being inspired by a mixture of both philosophies, they adopted a strategy of guerilla warfare.

The most influential ideologists of the religious forces who influenced big segments of the society (especially students) were Shariati and Jalal-e al-e Ahmad. Shariati was a Paris-educated sociologist whose works and views were highly influenced by Marxism and the idea of a just and classless society. He attempted to bring reform through Islamic thought and Shiism and believed that it would lead to a revolution and, ultimately, social justice. He was mainly popular among religious intellectuals.

Jalal-e al-e Ahmad was the other influential thinker and writer. He is most famous for introducing the concept of *Gharbzadegi* (westoxication), which was a critique of Western civilization and its implications on Iranian society. The concept emphasized nationalism, independence, and self-sufficiency. Anti-westoxication became part of the ideology of the revolution.

Among the secular groups, four organizations played a crucial role in the mobilization of the people:

1. The National Front: when Mosaadegh's government was overthrown by the 1953 coup, many members of the National Front were arrested. At that time, the National Front was unable to maintain an opposition against the Shah. In the early 1960s, however, during the period of liberalization, some of Mossadegh's followers established the Second National Front. But, by 1963, this had been repressed again. In 1977, the Shah increased its repression,

which provided an opportunity for oppositional organizations to re-start their activities and the Third National Front was established. The National Front had some supporters in the private sector and the bazaar. Outside the bazaar, its sympathizers included a small group of students, teachers, officers, some white collar employees, and professionals. However, it never gained the support of large numbers of people (see, e.g. Abrahamian 1982).

2. The Tudeh Party: although the Tudeh played a role during the revolution, after the 1953 coup and by the late 1950s, it was not very active. Apart from the enormous efforts of the government to destroy the Tudeh's reputation and influence, the party itself faced organizational challenges. Despite this, by the 1970s, Tudeh had many members in Europe and Iran, it had published a few newspapers, and had small underground cells at Tehran University, in the oil regions, and major industrial centers. Its most important contribution to the revolution was in organizing university protests and strikes, and, in the late revolutionary stage, to organize workers' strikes.

3. The Iranian People's Fadaiyan Guerilla: during the repressive years of 1962–63 some oppositional groups formed guerilla organizations. Among these, the Iranian People's Fada'iyan Guerilla had become famous. The organization was established in the mid-1960s by a group of young Marxist students, who split from the Tudeh Party and the National Front. They were inspired by the victory of Latin American guerillas, and, in 1971, they launched a guerilla program in the mountains of the north, which was unsuccessful. Most of the organization's supporters were university students (see Abrahamian 1982).

4. Writers' Association: the association was banned by the government shortly after it was founded in 1967. However, in 1977 it re-started activities. Within the revolutionary atmosphere of that time, the association attracted many people, mostly intellectuals from different political backgrounds and ideologies. Different political groups from liberals to Islamists and communists used to participate in the activities of the Writers' Association. Its most important contribution to mobilization was holding 16 poetry nights (mostly revolutionary poetry), at which thousands of people gathered.

The combination of different forces makes it clear that the revolutionary movement was not led by a single group or ideology, but by a heterogeneous and diverse group including bazaaris and clergy under the leadership of Khomeini, plus young educated people and leftist groups. The main aim of the revolution was summarized in a slogan repeated by the demonstrators all over the country: "Independence, Liberty, Islamic republic." However, none of these ideals were really clear or contextualized at that time. Antagonism towards the Shah was the most important common ground (Khosrokhavar 2004).

The long period of political repression had resulted in destruction of many political organizations, and therefore people had been deprived of political education. As Khosrokhavar (2004: 71) argues "they were not democratically minded." People were either influenced by the radical movements of the Islamic world, or by communist movements and guerillas of Latin America. Many urban poor and rural migrants who were not experienced with democracy, were taking part in the revolution because the populist slogans of Islam promised equality and justice. Moreover, because of the political repression there was an absence of strong political organizations, which made religious institutions such as mosques, Heyats (religious gathering during Muharram mourning month for the third Imam of Shia Muslims), etc., function as political parties. The ideology was Islam, with a focus on resistance to oppression and tyranny. Above all, Khomeini with his charismatic character, appeared as the leader of the masses who were looking for a hero to rescue them from dictatorship and repression (Amjad 1989).

The media played a major role in mobilizing the masses as well. Cassettes of Khomeini's speeches were distributed by people throughout the country. Moreover, the BBC played a crucial role in providing infor-mation all over the country during the revolution (Khosrokhavar 2004).

It has been argued that the movement faced five important phases prior to the last revolutionary stage (see, e.g. Ashraf and Banuazizi 1985; Daneshvar 1996).

The first phase (June–December 1977) was marked by non-violent protests and gatherings, which made the Shah liberalize the political scene to some extent. Therefore, the intelligentsia was more encouraged to participate in political protests and demonstrations. Different groups such as the National Front and the Tudeh Party re-organized their networks and activities. The Iranian Writers' Association organized nights of political poetry reading. Some petitions were circulated, and some open letters criticized the Shah.

The second phase (January–May 1978) was launched after a news-paper article against Khomeini appeared in *Ettelaat*, a very influential newspaper. The article claimed that Khomeini was an agent of a for-eign power whose aim was to destabilize the country. The clerics were irritated by the article. The bazaar and the seminaries in Qom (a holy city and the center of religious education in Iran) were closed in pro-test. Many people demonstrated on the streets, which led to violence and police interference. Nine people were killed during these protests. The memorial services held for them resulted in violent clashes in the city of Tabriz, in which a dozen people were killed. Forty days later, during a memorial service for those killed in Tabriz, security forces clashed with demonstrators in the city of Yazd.

The third phase (August–September 1978) was marked by mass demonstrations after 450 people were killed in a fire and explosion at the Rex Cinema in Abadan. The people blamed the fire on SAVAK (the intelligence service of the Shah). The Rex Cinema incident led to mobilization of the population of the oil region against the Shah.

By phase four (October–November 1978), white collar government employees, blue collar workers, students, and teachers were participating in the mass demonstrations. Moreover, all the major institutions experienced strikes, the Central Bank, the postal service, public utilities, hospitals, and ministries. Their demands varied from economics to politics. In mid-October, workers in the oil industry, the most important sector of the economy, went on strike. During this phase, the Shah was doing his best to satisfy the opposition, for example he cancelled the purchase of 70 F-14 Tomcat aircraft from the USA. He indicted the former head of SAVAK for torture of political prisoners and released all political prisoners. On 6 November, in a radio message to the nation, the Shah admitted to his past mistakes and promised that they would not be repeated. Throughout this phase, the US government also started to withdraw its support from the Shah.

The fifth phase (December 1978–February 1979) occurred when the Shah appointed a former member of the National Front, Shahpur Bakhtiar, as the prime minister and formed a council to discharge his constitutional duties in his absence. At the same time, Khomeini announced the formation of a Council of Islamic Revolution. The Shah left Iran, and Khomeini announced his plan of forming a provisional government and creating a new constitution. On 10 February, the Shah's guard was confronted by the revolutionary forces. The guard gave up on 12 February, and this resulted in the complete victory of the revolutionary forces.

On 30 and 31 March a referendum was held. With a result of 98 percent, Iranians voted for Iran to become an Islamic Republic. This was the end of the 2,500 years of monarchic rule in Iran.

The reform movement

Although a coalition comprising of different groups and ideologies began to emerge in the months after the victory of the revolution, the fundamentalists emerged as the dominant group by eliminating and/or weakening their opponents, under the leadership of Khomeini. In the very early stage of the post-revolutionary era, there was a period of 'multiple sovereignty' (Arjomand 1988: 135). However, by 1981 the clerics had monopolized the power and became the most powerful part of the regime.

Islam started to be considered an ideology with the potential to solve all of society's problems. Therefore, all aspects of Iranian society were being analyzed through Islamic ideology. Moreover, the concept of *vilayat-i faqih* (Guardianship of the Islamic Jurists) became part of the country's first constitution. This concept derives from a theory in Shia Islam, which believes that Islam gives the Islamic Jurist (*faqih*) custodianship over those in need of it. Moreover, Khomeini was declared as the sole *faqih*, the country's supreme jurist-consult. This meant that he was responsible for deciding whether the laws and modes of life in the society corresponded with Islamic principles (Ehteshami 1995). Furthermore, all the institutions of society were integrated into this power structure. The main objective was to establish an Islamic theocratic state based on a legal system and ideological control (Amjad 1988: 163). As Ehteshami (1995: 83) notes, "the new Islamic institutions emerged massively to control the private sphere of social life and civil society."

Moreover, the Iraqi invasion and the 8-year war from 1980 to 1988 empowered the Islamic regime because it united the Iranian society around it. Many Iranians considered Saddam Hussein not only their national enemy but also a religious enemy and an instrument of the West, which sought to eliminate the newly established Islamic Republic. The nationalist and religious feelings of being threatened by the West during the war made it easier for the Islamic regime to impose repression and suppress all movements against its hegemonic power (Khosrokhavar 2004).

Some policies of the new regime brought new benefits to the society. It spent a quarter of the annual budget in subsidies for bread, rice, sugar, cheese, fuel, and cooking oil, as well as indirect subsidies for electricity, sanitation, and piped water. Moreover, the percentage of children going to school rose from 60% to 90%, infant mortality per thousand dropped from 104 to 25, and the literacy rate doubled and illiteracy was almost eradicated among those in the age group 6-29 years. Thus, for the first time in the history of Iran, most of the population including different ethnicities (who speak other languages) could speak, read, and write in Persian (Abrahamian 2008: 180).

In general, Khomeini's era (1979–88) is marked by the Islamization of the country through an Islamic constitution, elimination of all oppositional groups, political repression, vast expansion of the public sector, the Iran–Iraq war (1980–8), weakening of the economy, and anti-Western foreign policy, especially anti-USA.[3]

After Khomeini's death, Khamenei was appointed as the *vali-e faqih*, and Rafsanjani became the president. This choice was made by Khomeini himself. Khamenei's effectiveness as a *faqih* and Rafsanjani's political reputation and pragmatism played a crucial role in the post-Khomeini era (see Kamrava 1992). This era has become known as "the reconstruction" era in the sociopolitical language of Iran.

After the war, Iran faced enormous problems, especially in economic terms. However, the war was not the only cause of the economic regression of Iran. Corruption, mismanagement, and insufficiency of many existing institutions, besides the damage caused by 8 years of war, all contributed strongly to the weak economic structures of that period (Ehteshami 1995).

Rafsanjani was a pragmatic leader, and started to implement policies to reverse the economic damage caused by the war. His main goals were to improve the primary infrastructure and increase economic growth. In order to achieve these goals, in contrast to the statist policies of the previous years, he started to liberalize the economy. His aim was to reconstruct the Iranian economy with the help of private, domestic, and foreign participation. Therefore, he favored a privatized, globalized, and free market system. Moreover, Rafsanjani, with Khamenei's support, eliminated all political opponents. None of the applications to form political parties, as authorized by the 1981 Parties Law, which was supposed to be put into practice after the war, were approved. Moreover, Rafsanjani arranged to have the Council of Guardians administer a competency exam in jurisprudence to candidates for the Assembly of Experts (see Ehteshami 1995).

Additionally, by scrutinizing those applying to run for the majlis and disallowing political opponents, the fourth majlis became dominated by supporters of Rafsanjani. Furthermore, it strengthened the position of a conservative, bazaar-backed group known as the Combative Clergy of Tehran Association, one of whose leaders, Nateq Nuri, became the speaker of the fourth majlis. Throughout the 1992–6 period this group won the support of Khamenei and penetrated the most important ministries of intelligence, culture, and Islamic guidance, and the interior ministry as well as the state media (Ehteshami 1995). Rafsanjani won the presidential election of 1993, and remained in office until 1997, when he was no longer eligible to run for president.

In general, under Rafsanjani's terms, society went through important transformations in culture and economy. The economy recovered from the war, with gross domestic product growing 8 percent per annum during 1988–93, and industry expanding close to 12 percent per year. Khatami (the future president) became the Minister of Culture and Islamic guidance. Although censorship of journals and films continued, Khatami was more moderate than his predecessors, and, as a result, the number of newspapers, journals, and films expanded rapidly. Moreover, as a consequence of new innovations in information technology, the internet was beginning to influence the societal life of Iranians. These changes, however, were very restricted, and freedom of expression and possibility of any association remained under control. Khatami was criticized for being too moderate in his administration of the Ministry of Culture and was dismissed in 1992 (see Ehteshami 1995).

In general, the country lacked pluralism under Rafsanjani and the important sections of the constitution related to freedom and liberty were neglected. The reason behind this is that implementation of these laws would have allowed political opponents to challenge the government. Executions of political opponents continued, and any organized political activity remained impossible. Moreover, all means of communication were controlled. The government's political strategists believed that by opening up economic channels the people would not demand political freedoms and reform (see Ehteshami 1995).

Furthermore, the anti-US policy of Rafsanjani paved the way for the Congress to pass the Iran Sanctions Act, which penalized American and foreign oil companies who invested more than 20 million dollars in Iran. The decrease in foreign investment, which coincided with a fall in oil prices from $20 per barrel in 1991 to $12 in 1994, added to Iran's external debt, leading to an economic recession. Consequently, unemployment increased, and the price of rice, sugar, and butter rose threefold, and that of bread sixfold (Abrahamian 2008: 185).

By 1997, the Islamic regime, which started as a populist theocracy, had been transformed to an oligarchy in which only a few institutions dominated the whole political establishment. There was a clear division between the so-called Islamic left and the clergy. The clergy was divided into two main political associations, which engaged in heated debates on Islamic ideology and republic. The Association of the Combatant Clergymen (*Ruhaniyun-e Mobarez*) was relatively liberal, whereas the Association of Combatant Clergy (*Ruhaniyat-e Mobarez*) was more traditional (Khosrokhavar 2004: 74).

The economic crisis, plus structural changes in state, society, and culture during the years after the revolution, paved the way for the reform movement to emerge. The claims and expectations of the large and educated middle class were very different from the early years of the revolution. After two decades of Islamic Republic rule, the dysfunction of the system was clear to the middle class. Moreover, the acceleration of globalization processes during the last decade of the twentieth century all over the world, and the collapse of many authoritarian regimes, had contributed to the growth of the concept of the civil society and democracy worldwide. These trends generated specific demands within different segments of society.

In the 1997 presidential election, over 200 candidates applied to run for president. However, the screening of the Guardian Council reduced the number to four, and among them only Nateq Nuri and Mohammad Khatami were strong candidates.

Nateq Nuri was a clergyman who, after serving in a few minor posts in the Islamic Republic, was elected to the majlis in 1986, and became its speaker. He was supported by the supreme leader Khamenei and many pro-revolutionary forces like *Basij* (a paramilitary force founded by Khomeini in 1979, which serves as an auxiliary force in moral policing and other religious activities).

Khatami, another member of the clergy was a lesser known figure in the political realm of Iran. He had served in various positions such as the Director of the Islamic Center in Hamburg, majlis Deputy and the Minister of Culture and Islamic Guidance under Rafsanjani's presidency. For his relaxation of censorship in the realm of cinema and press during his term as the Minister of Culture and Islamic Guidance, he became popular among intellectuals. Unlike Nuri, Khatami was seen as an outsider to the established political system and gained less attention during the electoral campaign from officials, especially the media.

However, his campaign organizers managed to stress themes such as "civil society," curing the "sick economy," "individual liberties," "women's rights," and "political pluralism." Furthermore, they emphasized that the philosophical books he had written had praised Western philosophy (Abrahamian 2008: 186).

On the day of the election 23 May 1997, astonishingly, 29.7 million—94 percent of eligible voters—went to the polls (compared with 16 million 4 years earlier). Khatami received 20.7 million votes (69 percent). He was most popular among youth and women. He was the first presidential candidate of Iran who officially emphasized the improvement of the status of women and addressed the needs of the young generation. Nateq Nuri received only 7 million votes. This event was a turning point in the sociopolitical life of modern Iran. By demonstrating that, unlike the Islamic character of all the institutions, millions of Iranians rejected the radical Islamic practices, it began a new chapter of social change and unrest. This proved conclusively that Iranians were dissatisfied with their situation, and that they favored change and reforms.

The reform movement was the result of deep structural changes in Iranian society and culture in the previous two decades of Islamic Republic rule. The core of the movement before the election day, as explained by Hamidreza Jalaipur (2003), a leading reformist, was not secular intellectuals, but followers of Khomeini during and after the revolution who were involved in the post-revolutionary politics of the country. They fought during the war, or were indirectly affected by it. With the conservative victory in occupying most of the political institutions, these people had been pushed out of the political system of Iran and disempowered. Many were students and followers of Abdolkarim Sorush, who played an important role in changing the conservative discourses of the post-revolutionary period to more pluralist discourses, despite being an influential ideologue of the Islamic Republic in its early years. Another group consisted of doctoral students of various disciplines who were sent to Europe, Canada, and Australia after the war. Although some of these intellectuals were originally followers of the revolutionary Islamic ideals at the beginning of the revolution, they concluded that the old and fanatical ideas of Islamic government were incapable of responding to the demands of the new society after experiencing the violent years after the revolution and war era. They demanded new discourses and debates, and they began to rethink all of the old notions to find a solution for the crisis of the Islamic government of Iran. However, all these intellectuals embraced the discourse of civil society, which was, at that time, a novel concept in Iranian society and politics (Khiabani and Sreberny 2001).

The leaders of the reform movement were, therefore, people who had been part of the dominant class within the Islamic government. Their success in promotion of their ideas among other segments of society through journals, newspapers, and lectures was because, unlike secular and atheist groups, they had been religious proponents of the revolution. Hence the conservatives could not, in the name of defending the values of Islam, revolution, and war, prohibit them from participating in politics. Thus, the election led to the emergence and growth of the reform discourse, despite the politically closed atmosphere (Jalaipur 2003).

One of the differences between the reformist leaders and the dominant religious groupings was that the reformists demanded equality on the basis of citizenship. However, the most important difference was the reformists' emphasis on the significance of civil society and the public sphere, although there was divergence among themselves in their understanding of civil society and its relations to the state. As Khiabani and Sreberny (2001) explained, some leaders of the reform movement were originally critical of state interference in all aspects of life, and they emphasized the importance of market forces. Others emphasized secularism, universalism, and the rationalization of social relations. For them, civil society meant overcoming traditions and the end of state interference in the private sphere. Another group opted for an end to the disorder in the political system, and demanded the restructuring of power in order to allow free expression of opinions and ideologies in a tolerant and pluralist context.

Although the reform movement has remained faithful to the Islamic character of the regime, its distinction from its conservative counterparts lies in the rejection of Islamic orthodoxy and fundamentalism as demanded by the conservatives. The reformists' aim is to replace the policy of "rejection and elimination" by a policy of "tolerance." Many reformists believe that there are different readings of Shia Islam, and they emphasize the freedom of individual thought and expression. That is why in the eyes of reformists, the word "republic" in the "Islamic Republic of Iran" is a crucial element, which demonstrates "popular sovereignty," whereas the element "Islamic," as also expressed by Khatami, is meant to be the unifier of the nation (Tabari 2003).

Apart from the religious intelligentsia, on the other side of the reform movement is the Iranian nation, which had experienced 2,500 years of monarchy before the revolution. Although Iranian people demanded liberty and freedom of thought after the revolution of 1979, they had to live through the dark years of the post revolution, in which their demands went unfulfilled. Apart from the 8-year war, the people had to tolerate extreme repression and censorship. Therefore, although the core of the movement's support were the Islamic leftists, many members of the modern middle class, college students, women, and urban workers also supported the reform movement (Abrahamian 2008: 186). Furthermore, many of the poor and economically disenfranchised sections of society also supported the ideas of building a civil society and guaranteeing individual rights. Therefore, Khatami's electoral victory was the result of a coalition that included millions of women, youth, intellectuals, journalists, artists, clergy, and technocrats who dreamt of a different society (Yaghmaian 2002).

As Alavitabar (2001: 57) explains, at the dawn of the reform movement society faced three different dualisms: non-secularism/secularism, tradition/modernity, and democracy/despotism.

What made the 20 million Iranians vote for Khatami and not his opponent Nuri who was receiving extreme support from the state? The answer to this question requires an in-depth analysis of the socio-political situation in Iran before the election, as well as the psychological characteristics of the election campaign and the voters. But, in short, what has played the most important role in the flourishing of a reform movement has certainly been the emergence of a "united yes" to new values of civil society and political reform, rule of law, freedom, and democracy, and a "united no" to totalitarianism and Islamic fundamentalism. Rejection of Nuri (as the symbol of the ruling system) was a rejection of the whole system. The people demonstrated that they no longer identified themselves with the system, and demanded structural changes. The election made it clear that Iranians' expectations go beyond the limitations of a theocratic dictatorship. Moreover, it represented the demand of the majority of people for the ideals of tolerance, moderation, respect for diversity, and dialogue as was repeatedly emphasized by Khatami during his electoral campaign. People viewed Khatami as a person who could signal change and liberalize the political system.

In sum, a few factors can be counted as explanations for the victory of Khatami and the reform movement (see Jalaipur 2003). First, Khatami's promises to improve the economy and to provide more job opportunities. But these were not new promises, as Rafsanjani's campaign focused on similar issues.

Second, the absence of any discourse of democracy for almost 20 years, and the objection of many officials to this discourse, led to the unification of millions of people from different ideologies and backgrounds in favor of reform.

Third, Nuri supported the old discourse of social conservatism, which had been the dominant discourse for two decades. Khatami, on the other hand, had influence among the educated middle class, intellectuals, and students, and they supported reform rather than conservatism.

The final reason was the partially free Iranian political life, with relatively free elections, and equal voting rights for women. This maintained a high level of civic participation in political life, especially in presidential elections. People realized that the 1997 election was a watershed because for the first time in many years the candidates represented two different ideologies and programs. For this reason, many Iranians who rarely voted or were or reluctant to participate in the Islamic Republic's elections, went to the polls and cast a ballot.

The largest numbers of votes for Khatami were cast by youth. As the voting age in Iran was 15 years of age during the 1997 election (since January 2007 Iran has increased the voting age to 18), and more than half of the population of Iran was younger than 25, the views of this age group who did not experience the pre-revolutionary years were not shaped by revolutionary ideals (Tabari 2003).

In the aftermath of the victory of the reform movement, society and politics underwent striking transformations. Spectacular victories followed the 1997 triumph: the reformists obtained 75 percent of the vote in local elections in 1999, when 334,000 candidates, including some 5,000 women, competed for 115,000 seats on provincial, town and village councils; in parliamentary elections in 2000, the reformists won 80 percent of the vote and obtained 195 of the 290 majlis seats; and in 2001 Khatami won a second term as president, receiving 80 percent of all votes cast (Abrahamian 2008: 188). As Khosrokhavar (2004) claimed, "since 1997, a stalemate has prevailed: the society is post Islamist, whereas the decisive power centers are controlled by Islamist conservatives." Victory by Ahmadinezhad and his conservative front since 2005, however, led to a new period of political repression and change in power structures.

For the 2009 presidential elections a broad coalition of pro-reform Iranians launched a campaign called the "Third Wave," with the goal of winning a third presidential term for Mohammad Khatami. Repression of the reform movement under the restrictive atmosphere imposed by Ahmadinezhad's government was the main motivation of the Third Wave campaign. After holding many seminars, workshops, lectures, etc., attended by large audiences, on 8 February 2009, Khatami announced that he would run in the 2009 presidential election. However, on 16 March he withdrew from the race, and supported the campaign of his long-time friend and advisor, the former prime minister, Mir-Hossein Musavi.

Ten days before the 10th presidential election Musavi and Ahmadinezhad (the two most important candidates of the election) engaged in a heated debate on live television, which was watched by millions of Iranians. Thousands of people rallied and celebrated in the streets of Tehran, confident that Musavi and his reformist agenda would win the election. Astonishingly, supporters of other candidates joined the street rallies in subsequent days.

The shocking result of the presidential election of 12 June 2009 and the so-called victory of Mahmud Ahmadinezhad led to a new chapter of social change and unrest. Millions of people who participated in the presidential election in support of the reform movement felt betrayed by the supposed election fraud of the Islamic Republic. The post-election months marked the most remarkable outpouring of demonstrators and street fighters across the country since the revolutionary days of 1979. After 1 week, however, the mass protests stopped, due to immense pressure from military and para-military forces. A few weeks later, however, on the anniversary of the student uprising of 1999, people again demonstrated in masses to protest against the election results. For a period of time, the streets of Tehran and other big cities were sites of frequent mass demonstrations and rallies. Moreover, the gap between the reformists and the conservatives started to widen. This increasing fragmentation within the political system goes hand in hand with the ongoing and intensified resistance of Iranians for democracy and freedom, and is paving the way for further developments. However, the direction these developments might take still remains unclear and the political situation is highly unpredictable.

Nonetheless, what is apparent is that Iran has entered a new phase of struggle and unrest. The 2009 uprising emerged within the framework of the reform movement, hence it carries the same characteristics. However, apart from the unique mass protests and the ever-increasing conflict between reformists and conservatives (and in some cases even among the conservatives themselves), two other prominent distinctions of this phase of uprising are as follows.

First, the widespread use of the internet as a communication and mobilization tool: after attempts by the government to limit traditional tools of communication in Iran, the reformists found novel ways of communicating. They started blogging, posting videos on You tube, starting Facebook groups, and mobilizing their protests and demonstrations with Twitter. Moreover, as journalists and foreign media faced restrictions, ordinary people used the internet to send pictures and videos of demonstrations to news agencies.

Second, the presence of women: although women have been playing an important role in the reform movement from its very beginning, during and after the 2009 election their presence in the movement, and especially the mass protests and demonstrations, increased dramatically. Moreover, for the first time in the history of Iran, a candidate's wife (Zahra Rahnavard), actively participated during the electoral campaign, and she has been playing an important role in the uprising after the election. Rahnavard has been continuously encouraging Iranian women to stand up for their rights. Also, Neda Aghasoltan, a young Iranian woman who was shot dead during the mass protests, became a symbol of the female Iranian protesters. After her dramatic death, which was filmed and syndicated by news agencies within hours, protestors began carrying her picture at almost all demonstrations, and chanting slogans such as: "We are all Neda."

Continuity or detachment?

An overview of the first three movements in this chapter, i.e. the constitutional movement, the national oil movement and the revolutionary movement of 1979, demonstrates that Iranian society has faced cycles of social movement uprising during the last century. Moreover, it reveals that all three movements followed a similar pattern and shared common characteristics. This pattern can be summarized as follows.

The movements have been the consequence of different paths of modernization in each period. Changes have occurred in the economic, social, and intellectual structures of each era, bringing new demands and expectations. At the same time, society was experiencing a heavy presence of foreign influence and domination. Moreover, at each stage of the movements' uprising, the political system had been suppressing political opposition for a long time, and discontent with the government had been growing among different segments of society, especially the middle class. Therefore, the state–society relationship had never improved and had always been problematic. All movements emerged in periods of sluggish political liberalization, combined with the onset of an economic crisis. There was similarity in the social structure and composition of each movement; in each case there was a coalition of the modern middle class (intelligentsia) and traditional middle class (ulama + bazaaris), which led to the formation of different identities, groups, and classes in the later stages of the movements. However, all movements became nationwide and ultimately transcended class movements. The main goals of all three movements were implementation of a democratic system and independence from foreign influences. As Poulson (2006: 303) explains, debates concerning national sovereignty (how the Iranian state should achieve independence in the world), and individual sovereignty (the rights individual Iranians have in their political and social system) have been dominant debates of the previous movements. On the one hand, the past social movements sought to end Western imperialism, and, on the other hand, to defend the rights that individual Iranians would need in their political system. However, the absence of a strong public sphere and civil society to institutionalize the demands of the public through mediating institutions led to the failure of these movements, and subsequently to new eras of repression.

The reform movement has followed most of the previous patterns, although it has been different in some aspects. It emerged as a consequence of modernization and structural changes during the post-revolution period, the emergence of a large and highly educated middle class, economic chaos of the post-revolutionary era, repression within the political system, and absence of civil society organizations. Moreover, an economic crisis followed the economic liberalization of the state, shortly before the emergence of the movement.

However, a few differences characterize the reform movement from earlier movements. First, although previous movements were driven to violence in their late stages, the reform movement has developed new ways of struggling against the systemic problems. Non-violent methods have been adopted. The focus on "reform," "dialogue," and "institutionalization of democracy" has made it a movement that seeks slow and profound changes rather than rapid and hasty transformations. The reform movement does not pursue social change through a single program but through various means, such as citizen participation and the creation of civil society organizations. Even since the June 2009 uprising and the attempt by the government to channel reformist protests in a violent direction, leaders and followers of the movement have done their best to follow their goals through non-violent protests, sometimes referring to Gandhi's non-violent resistance.[4] In addition to silent demonstrations, symbolic actions such as using the color green as an icon for supporters of Musavi (the Iranian national football team wore green armbands in support of Musavi during a World Cup qualifying match), and nightly roof protests calling "Down with Dictator" and "God is Great," are examples of non-violent and symbolic protests. Interestingly, nightly roof protests in which residents repeatedly shout "God is Great" was a tactic developed during the revolution of 1979. Although religion was not the main concern of the protestors in the reform movement, the symbolic action of repeating the famous ritual of 30 years ago had a significant revolutionary message.

Furthermore, unlike previous movements, there was no coalition of modern middle class and traditional middle class in the reform movement. Until the recent uprising of the movement in June 2009 after the election fraud, the movement's supporters were mostly from the educated segments of the middle class. The traditional middle class, i.e. bazaaris and most of the ulamas, maintained their conservative political positions. Since June 2009, there also has been pro-reform support from some segments of the traditional middle class and the lower class. In other words, the Green Movement has gone nationwide and beyond its middle class origin. However, its core still remains the modern middle class.

Nevertheless, the clergy is divided into two main political groups: a group of combatant clergy considered reformist (*Ruhaniyun-e Mobarez*), and a group of combatant clergy that are conservative and oppose the reform movement (*Ruhaniyat-e Mobarez*). In other words, the ulamas have not acted as a coherent social group. Since June 2009 the conflict between these two groups has increased dramatically.

Moreover, whereas one of the past social movements' main aims was to establish independence from foreign powers, the activists of the reform movement seek to establish a conciliatory dialogue with the West (see Chapter 3). Emergence of this new discourse among the new social activists, however, is not identical with full acceptance of the West. Instead, it is oriented towards interaction with the West in a manner that does not threaten the identity of Iranians (Poulson 2006).

The most dramatic distinction, however, is the change that has occurred in the 'master framework' of the movement. Master frameworks are specific themes around which a movement's ideas are clustered (Poulson 2006). Although still organized around debates concerning "national sovereignty" and "individual sovereignty," the reform movement

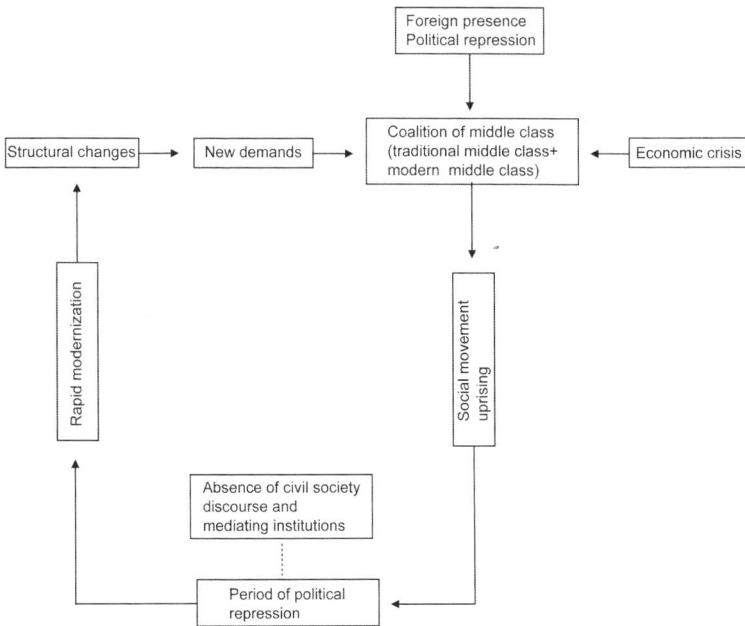

Figure 2.1 Cycles of social movement uprising in twentieth-century Iran (before the emergence of the reform movement)

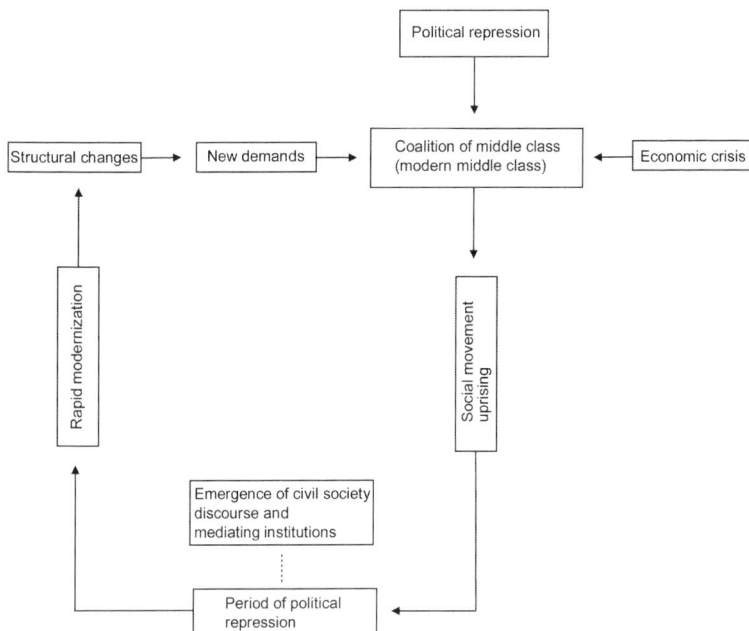

Figure 2.2 Uprising of the reform movement

became a movement for the recognition of a public sphere, civil society, and citizenship rights (it is important to mention that an indirect goal of all previous social movements has been to empower civil society vis-à-vis the state, but expanding the boundaries of civil society was never an explicit goal of any of these movements). So, within the framework of individual sovereignty, a new public discourse has emerged (see Chapter 3). Moreover, it demonstrates the emergence of new kinds of social activists who have new demands and needs. The reform movement has new understandings of power relations and the state–society relationship. This is mainly represented in the rise of new discourses, narratives, and forms of resistance.

Conclusion

This chapter investigated how Iranian grand social movements started, changed, and developed over time. Iranians began the twentieth century with the constitutional movement, and ended the century with the reform movement. As was shown, social movements are not discrete events, but instead there has been continuity and dynamism as they

first layer

frameworks of 'national' and 'individual' sovereignty

second layer

new discourses, narratives, counter narratives and new forms of resistance

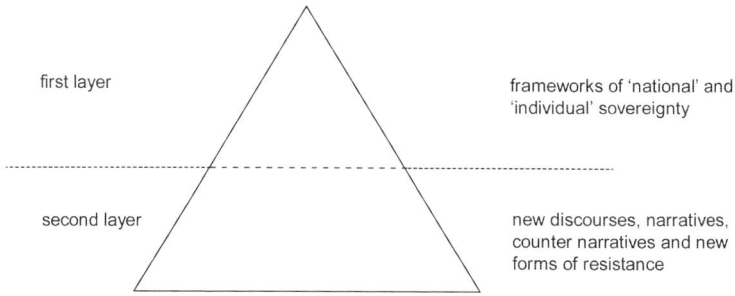

Figure 2.3 Two layers of the reform movement

have constantly evolved. This helps us understand and analyze the current movements as extensions of previous movements and not as isolated entities.

However, the emergence of the reform movement in the closing years of the millennium has opened a new chapter for Iranian social movements. The most notable transformation has been the "two-layered" characteristic of the reform movement. On the one hand, the reform movement follows the earlier movements' master frameworks, i.e. frameworks of "national sovereignty" and "individual sovereignty," whereas, on the other hand, emphasis on the discourses of the public sphere and civil society has given rise to the emergence of a new layer within the movement. This has led to the formation of new discourses, narratives, counternarratives, and new forms of resistance.

This "two-layered" facet provides a context for understanding the emergence of a set of new actors, and forms of action (including environmental movement), which were followed by the reform movement. The fundamental changes that occurred in the aftermath of the reform movement, will be argued in detail in the following chapter.

3 Civil society discourse as the battleground of societal change

Introduction

The reform movement introduced new debates and discourses into Iranian society. Abrahamian (2008: 186) describes how the movement changed key terms of the public discourse, from "martyrdom," "revolution," and "westoxication," to "democracy," "pluralism," "liberty," "equality," "civil society," "human rights," "political participation," "citizenship," etc. Above all, the rise of the civil society discourse (sphere of the society in which movements, groups, and self-organized social forces independent from the state and market, work to mediate political power), and its relationship to the state and among Iranian politicians, and in Iranian social life gained specific attention. The rise of this new discourse established a new sphere of public life, and paved the way for emergence of new kinds of civic activities. It has become a battleground on which different conflicts and movements have been played out.

The first objective of this chapter is to illustrate these new trends. The second objective is to provide an analysis of the current status of Iranian civil society, as the synthesis of the Khatami and post-Khatami eras. Finally, the chapter aims to provide a framework for the newly emerged environmental movement, which is analyzed in depth in the following chapter.

The nature and development of civil society in contemporary Iran

Although the structure and nature of the state in Iran has always been undemocratic and left little space for civil society, in specific periods there have been organizations that exploited the boundaries of what was tolerated by the state.

Establishing an open civil society has been the ultimate aim of Iranian social activists for at least the last 100 years. During the last century an indirect goal of the social movements from constitutional revolution to the national oil movement and the 1979 revolution, was to change or empower the civil society. Although, at times, Iranian civil society has been dynamic, most of the time it has been repressed.

The modern public sphere in Iran emerged at the beginning of the twentieth century, along with the emergence of the modern nation-state. The public sphere was mostly evident in the founding of independent and critical newspapers and journals, as well as rapidly growing voluntary associations and societies (Katouzian 2003: 105).

Secret societies (*anjomans*), which started at the beginning of the century, along with the constitutional movement, were spaces of intellectual gathering where new ideas and themes were discussed. Most of the *anjomans'* activities were focused on modern themes and social and political issues. Membership in these *anjomans* was commonly secret because of the radical nature of themes and concepts that were being discussed. The state often considered them a threat. After the coup of 1953, *anjomans* and most independent organizations, political parties, councils, etc. were either banned or strictly controlled (Abrahamian 1982).

Although in the beginning the main goal of the 1979 revolution was to establish a democratic system, as the revolution achieved a measure of success the dominant discourse became the revolution itself. Many people believed that the Shah should leave, and any alternative system of government would be better. There was no clear idea of what would come next. As a result, during 1979, from the victory of the revolution until the complete establishment of the Islamic republic, the dominant discourse of society was the revolutionary discourse.

After the victory of the revolution, political freedom and an open public sphere for independent newspapers, associations, organizations, political parties, councils, etc., were key demands of the people and they were eventually enshrined in the constitution. Nevertheless, political repression soon resumed, and the 8-year war with Iraq and its consequences did not provide a sphere for civil liberties. Independent institutions of social, political, and cultural life were destroyed. As a result, all kinds of grassroots organizations and political parties, which were formed or became active during the temporary and relative political freedom of the revolutionary period of 1978–9, were dissolved and banned. The universities were invaded by security forces, and members of student and faculty associations were arrested and, occasionally, executed. Newspaper headquarters and book stores were ransacked and books were burned. An all-inclusive system of censorship and terror was launched by the state to avoid any manifestation of public and collective thoughts and actions (Yaghmaian 2002).

The years followed by the revolution marked the elimination of all opposition groups. Maintaining the revolutionary discourse was a key strategy of the state as a means to mobilize people during the Iran–Iraq war. Consequently, these years were characterized by the dominance of a "conservative" discourse. The attempt was to avoid any polarization or fragmentation within the polity, and the government exercised a high degree of control over the society.

The end of the war coincided with the collapse of Soviet Union and the re-emergence of the concept of civil society as a tool for understanding the changes that occurred in Eastern European societies. It was during this time that the concept was introduced into Iranian popular politics.

The reform movement started gradually after the end of the war with Iraq and Khomeini's death. This period has been called "the second republic," as the society and state underwent prominent changes. Under Khomeini's guidance, Iran experienced a period marked by policies of integration of the executive and legislature with clerical authorities. Moreover, during the 8-year war, Iran had no choice but to be condemned to political, diplomatic, and economic conditions of the war era (Ehteshami 1995).

After the war, because of the easing of revolutionary emotions and ideologies, the importance of civil institutions and their independence from the state became clearer. Therefore, during this period Iran experienced a slow political liberalization.

One of the characteristics of modern societies is independence of institutions and organizations, and many Muslim intellectuals who had been part of the dominant power bloc in the early years after the revolution started to realize that the conservative ideals of the post-revolutionary era were no longer responsive to the new needs of society. New approaches and discourses were required in order to cope with new demands of the changing society. The civil society discourse first emerged in the 1990s among Muslim intellectuals, and it was later popularized among many other segments of society. Although its development was slow and weak in the beginning, it became the dominant discourse during the electoral campaign and after the 1997 presidential election (Jalaipur 2003).

Before the revolution of 1979, Iran experienced decades of Westernization; however, culture and society were only exposed to superficial aspects of Western civilization. The years after the revolution were characterized by isolation and repression. Khatami's era was the first time in the history of that society experienced an accelerated promotion of civil institutions nationwide and opened up to Islamic Republic (Seddighi 2001:16). Additionally, it was an era in which public participation and critical debate, open discussion, public sphere, civil society, institutionalization of democracy, pluralism, and the rights of individuals had taken root as never before in Iran. In general, the era introduced Iranian society to previously unknown concepts and discourses. From 1997 to 2005, Iranian civil society organizations (CSOs) emerged in many different social spheres, and they experienced frequent rises and falls. During his election campaign and throughout his presidency, Khatami's most important rhetoric was to establish a vibrant civil society.

Throughout the hundred years of the history of the modern state in Iran, there have always been individuals or groups who could act beyond the boundaries of law. However, Khatami's main concern was the reinforcement of civil society institutions through constitutional law and to make civil activities part of the legal rights of citizens. He repeatedly stressed the importance of individual sovereignty and individual rights.

Although in many respects Khatami referred to civil society according to Muslim cultural norms, his acquaintance with Western thinkers makes his conception of civil society indistinguishable from that of the Western civil society (Poulson 2005: 255). In the following speech given at the Islamic summit conference in 1997, he recognized both Muslim and Western forms of civil society:

We can certainly move the present as well as the future generation towards the new Islamic civilization through setting our eyes on horizons farther away, being together with understanding and helping each other as brothers. For this to become a reality, all of us must dedicate ourselves to the realization of the 'Islamic civil society' in our respective countries. The civil society which we want to promote and perfect in our society and which we recommend to other Islamic societies is fundamentally different from the civil society that is rooted in the Greek philosophical thinking and Roman political tradition, and which having gone through the Middle Ages, has acquired its peculiar orientation and identity in the modern world. The two, however, are not necessarily in conflict and contradiction in all their manifestations and consequences. This is exactly why we should never be oblivious to judicious acquisition of the positive accomplishments of the Western civil society.

(Khatami 9 December 1997)

Although the reform movement officially started within the government, the creation of a more open society has paved the way for others to try and establish new discourses or forms of resistance from outside the circle of power. Moreover, the reform movement undermined the legitimacy of the regime and some of its important institutions in the eyes of many Iranians, especially the educated middle class (Tabari 2003).

In general, in the aftermath of the reform movement, two different major groups have contributed to the opening up of society. The first is the religious intellectuals who, through philosophical and theological hermeneutics rooted in Islam and Shiism, seek to introduce new values, and undermine the sacred theological structures of the Islamic Republic. The other group has a secular background, define themselves through non-religious means and goals, and are dominant in Iranian culture, i.e. Iranian cinema, theater, novel writing, poetry, painting, etc. These two groups are in constant interaction with each other, and the former is highly influenced by the latter as well as Western philosophical thoughts (Khosrokhavar 2004). In some instances, such as in the press and the new social movements, these two groups work together.

Even though not completely independent from the state, the newly emerged discourse of civil society has contributed to the construction of novel discourses, narratives and counternarratives, new forms of political resistance, and social movements in society. The following is a brief overview of the newly emerged discourses, narratives, counternarratives and resistances:

1. Dialogue among civilizations (new discourse)

In response to Samuel Huntington's (1996) theory of the clash of civilizations, Khatami has introduced the idea of "dialogue among civilizations." He believes that through such a dialogue realization of universal justice and liberty can be initiated, and that the establishment and development of civility depends on dialogue among societies and civilizations with different values and approaches (see Khatami *et al.* 2001: 18).

The term was made famous after the United Nations accepted the Iranian delegation's suggestion to name the year 2001, as the year of "dialogue among civilizations." Unlike the conservatives, Khatami believes that a world culture has emerged and that civilizations always interact with each other:

> What we ought to consider in earnest today, is the emergence of a world culture. World culture cannot and ought not to overlook

characteristics and requirements of native local cultures, with the aim of imposing itself upon them. Cultures and civilizations that have naturally evolved among various nations in the course of history are constituted from elements that have gradually adapted to collective souls and to historical and traditional characteristics. As such, these elements cohere with each other and consolidate within an appropriate network of relationships.

(Khatami *et al.* 2001: 31)

Apart from the international approval of the concept, Iranian people also have enthusiastically accepted the new discourse. It attracted the attention of the Iranian society because of the similarities between Huntington's theory and the dominant ideology of the conservatives in Iran in recent years. Similar to Huntington, the conservatives believe that there is a fundamental conflict between Western civilization and Islamic civilization, and that they will remain hostile enemies. Khatami's proposal for "dialogue" instead of "clash," met with hostility from conservatives, whereas it received full acceptance from other segments of the society (Poulson 2005).

2. The re-rise of Islamic modernism (counternarrative)

The term Islamic modernism mostly refers to the relationship between "Islam" and "modernity," and the ways in which they interact. Islamic modernism emerged as a counternarrative to the Islamic fundamentalist narrative of the post-revolution years. The history of Islamic modernism in Iran goes back to the Qajar era, and the dawn of the constitutional revolution. However, it did not gain influence in the public discourse until shortly before the revolution of 1979, when Shariati's interpretation of Islam as a counterhegemonic articulation against the clergy's interpretation of Islam, as well as an alternative to the leftist's revolutionary ideologies, became one of the leading ideologies of the revolution of 1979 (Ghamari-Tabrizi 2004). Islamic modernism attracted many students and intellectuals of the pre-revolutionary era.

As the Pahlavi regime was strictly against any kind of Marxist associations and activities, the Islamic modernists gained popularity among many segments of society, especially university students. During the final years of the Pahlavi regime, the Islamic modernists became popular and they ultimately took power in the newly established regime. After a short period, however, Islamic fundamentalists were able to seize power and the Islamic modernists were sidelined. The reform movement allowed for the emergence of a public sphere in which Islamic ideas could be discussed and criticized. It paved the way for a re-rise of Islamic modernism, which was a return to the modernist perspectives of pre-revolution Muslim intellectuals.

Abdolkarim Sorush, the pioneer of the Islamic modernism after the revolution, claims that there are perennial unchanging religious truths, but our understanding of them is dependent on our knowledge in the fields of science and philosophy. He believes that there is a difference between religion that is divinely revealed, and the interpretation of religion or religious knowledge based on sociohistorical factors (Ghamari-Tabrizi 2004).

Hassan Yussefi Eshkevari, an Iranian cleric, is one of the most influential critics of the Iranian version of theocracy, and he stands for the separation of religion and state. He supports reform of Islamic thought in order to make it compatible with the needs of a modern society. He was among the prominent Iranian intellectuals, who attended the "Iran after the Election Conference" in Berlin. At this conference he stated:

> The experiences of the last twenty years have proved that freedom, democracy and citizenship are prerequisites of any kind of social, cultural, political and economic development.
>
> (Yussefi Eshkevari 2001: 35)

And:

> Even if Khatami should be defeated in his work, this time not only has democracy become the first priority, but there is an unprecedented consensus among the intellectual and the political elites. The historical time of despotism is over in Iran.
>
> (Quoted in Mir-Hosseini and Tapper 2006: 180)

Mohammad Mojtahed Shabestari, a cleric who is a professor of philosophy and theology at Tehran University, stresses that religion is not capable of organizing a modern society. He argues that a state based on the traditional reading of religion is not democratic and it violates the basics of human rights (Yaghmaian 2002).

David Hirts (1997), in his report about political changes in Iran post 1997, referring to Jalaipur, a theorist and a leading figure of the reform movement who served in different official positions during the post-revolutionary years, writes that the reformists do not believe that religion can offer a modern program for society, and that the institutional separation of religion and the state is necessary.

3. Rise of critical newspapers, journals, and books (new form of resistance)

A few months after the election of Khatami, licenses were issued for many newspapers and journals. This was mostly because greater press freedom had been one of Khatami's promises. The relaxation of censorship fostered a free press, which played an important role in informing the public of alternative views. Moreover, in the absence of diverse political parties, the newly emerged publishing sphere played an important role in organizing social movements and supporting nongovernmental organizations (NGOs). The critical press could articulate the voices of social agents, which were not allowed to express themselves under the previous regime, and those who were willing to create the institutions of their collective voice. As Behzad Yaghmaian (2002: 4) explains, "the critical press became the voice of the civil society in the making."

In just 1 year, between 1998 and 1999, licenses for 168 new publications including seven daily newspapers, 27 weeklies, 59 monthlies, 53 quarterlies, and two annual publications were issued (Khiabani and Sreberny 2001). This marked a dramatic change in the regulation of the Iranian press, which was followed by the easing of censorship of books. Eventually, the press became the most active section of the newly emerged civil society.

The first Iranian newspaper *Vaqaye-e Ettefaqieh*, was published in the middle of the nineteenth century following reforms implemented by Nasir al-Din Shah's reformist prime minister Amir Kabir. However, his short rule did not lead to the institutionalization of a free press. By the end of the century, following another set of reforms and the subsequent dawn of the constitutional movement, more newspapers were published. These newspapers sought to introduce new concepts and discourses such as "freedom" and "democracy." They played an important role during the constitutional movement (Zibakalam 2004).

In the years after the constitutional revolution, some of the emerged constitutionalist newspapers continued to be published and some were replaced by new newspapers. During this period, Iran lacked a central government and faced a civil war. Therefore, the newspapers' main goals were to publicize the inefficiency of the governors and oppose foreign interference (Zibakalam 2004).

Under Reza Shah, only a few newspapers could bear the despotic atmosphere of his reign (many of the newspapers were banned, and many journalists were attacked, arrested, and jailed). After the fall of Reza Shah, a more open sociopolitical atmosphere developed, and consequently the numbers of newspapers and magazines rose dramatically. However, after the coup of 1953 until the revolution of 1979, the press remained under state control, and was an important mouthpiece for the Shah's regime (Zibakalam 2004).

After the Iranian revolution of 1979, the press remained under private ownership, but was tightly controlled by the state. Under Rafsanjani, a few more privately owned periodicals were published. However, they operated under strict control of the relevant ministries, such as the Ministry of Islamic Culture and Guidance and the Ministry of Information (Khiabani and Sreberny 2001).

During Khatami's presidency, the newly published newspapers were trying to go beyond the Islamic clichés of the previous newspapers, which were strictly controlled by the state. Many newspapers and journals specialized in women, youth, politics, culture, etc. They were critical of the prevailing political system, and the religious behavior of the fundamentalists, while advocating the ideals of the reform movement and the new ideas of democracy, civil society, and freedom. The press became a platform for the production of new ideas and the frontier of civil society in a country where the channels of information and the public manifestation of thoughts have been strictly censored for many years.

The first newspaper of this kind, called *Jameeh* (society), became famous as "the first newspaper of the Iranian civil society." After a few volumes it became a free platform for ideological discussions between different groups. It created a critical atmosphere, in which many thinkers and ordinary people could express their ideas for the first time in the history of Iranian newspapers. Although it was only published for 3 months, *Jameeh* was read by more than 300,000 (Jalaipur 2003) intellectuals, students, and citizens. This was a turning point in the history of the Iranian press.

However, after the presidential election of 1997 it was not only the number of newspapers and journals that increased dramatically but also many books that had been waiting for approval from the Ministry of Culture were also published. Through newspapers, journals, and books, critical ideas and themes, even some criticism of the regime, started to be released publicly.

On 12 June 2005, shortly before the ninth presidential election, in a speech held in the province of Khuzestan, Khatami emphasized the importance of the development of a critical discourse as one of the main achievements of his presidency, and he said that "voicing criticisms is no longer considered as an act against the security of the country" (Payvand News Agency 2005).

A telling sign that signaled the ongoing struggle of civil society and the reform movement, was the fact that the closure of each newspaper was followed by the launch of a new newspaper of the same kind. Moreover, the easing of press censorship was also followed by the popularization of critical ideas focused on citizenship rights, and the importance of an active civil society. In some cases books directly criticized the current theocratic system. They called for its replacement with secular democracy. Furthermore, translations of Western critical theory, philosophy, sociology, arts, etc., helped foster an intellectual culture that challenged the dominant hegemonic ideology of the Islamic regime (Yaghmaian 2002: 119).

4. Emergence of citizenship discourse in response to the discourse of *khodi* versus *gheyre khodi*—from us versus not from us (new discourse)

One of the most undemocratic ideas that became part of the Islamic Republic's political discourse since the late 1980s, has been the idea of classifying Iranian citizens as *khodi*, i.e. people who believe in the ideology of the government, and *gheyre khodi*, i.e. people who have a critical mindset towards the ideology of the regime. *Khodi* (from us) refers to people who are in total agreement with the ideology and method of government. This group is a minority of the population but benefits from the social and political structures of the Islamic Republic, and has a chance of entering the elite strata of society that controls the economy and politics. *Gheyre khodi* (not from us) refers to all other groups and ideologies that are not in harmony with the Islamic Republic, although some believe in the Islamic constitution. These are the majority of people and include many different ideologies (Marxists, Liberals, ordinary people, etc.). This group is practically excluded from effective decision making. This has created a political structure that interacts with people purely in regard to their stance towards the dominant ideology of the Islamic Republic, irrespective of the constitution and law.

Before the reform movement there was no prominent opposition within the government, and no oppositional group outside the government was tolerated. Therefore, this classification had led to the polarization of the society into two opposing groups: a minority within the government who are absolutely loyal to the ideological construction of the government, and the majority who are in some way opposed to this ideology. This includes those totally against the regime, as well as those who demand reforms and transformation within the same structure.

One of the most important slogans of the reform movement has been "Iran for all Iranians." This slogan emphasizes the importance of "citizenship" and "individual rights," rather than ideological beliefs. Under this discourse, individuals and groups, regardless of their ideologies and within the framework of the constitution, have the opportunity to work, cooperate and compete for their political demands while their rights are upheld. This has been an important progression in fulfilling the promises of a civil society under the reform movement.

5. Construction of democracy discourse within the public sphere (new discourse)

The ultimate goal of most authoritarian regimes is to control the direction of thoughts and prohibit the generation of different voices and social resistances. In an authoritarian society, a public sphere for circulation of thoughts either does not exist, or is strictly controlled. As control was relaxed under Khatami, democracy became one of the central elements of the public sphere's discourse. Within the flourishing intellectual atmosphere of universities, cafes, meetings, lectures, web logs, etc., democracy became one of the main themes of many lectures, discussions, articles, and resistances. This emerging discourse started to pose a major challenge to the undemocratic political structure of the regime.

6. Rise of CSOs and new movements (new forms of resistance)

Khatami's era marked the awakening period of CSOs, whose concern was to contribute to a more democratic society. During this period, different social groups saw an opportunity to organize themselves as CSOs, in spite of the existing constraints and limitations. Since then, Iranian CSOs have grown and emerged in different social spheres, albeit in fits and starts.

These collective actions aimed to change Iranians' expectations of the state–society relationship, and the definition of democracy, human rights, environment, women, student, children, youth, etc. Some CSOs also managed to become highly organized, establishing a for example a Teacher's Guild, Journalist's Guild, etc. Although each group and organization has its own mission, they all campaign for reforms in political, social, and cultural spheres. In other words their actions seek to influence the state and the society, by pursuing a shift in social, political and cultural norms. These activists represent different social groups, and address a variety of issues. According to official figures (produced by the Statistics Center of the Islamic Republic of Iran), there were 6,914 NGOs in Iran in 2004 (Razzaghi 2007).

Furthermore, as a consequence of emergence of information society in the past 10 years, the use of the internet has grown significantly in Iran. Iranian social activists have created a virtual civil society using the internet. The virtual civil society has become a sphere of discussion and expression of new thoughts and ideas. It is getting bigger every day and attracting more and more people.

Although still facing many constraints from existing laws and authoritarian sections of the government, civil society activists have found their own ways of entering into dialogue with government authorities and different entities of civil society. This has allowed room for citizen participation.

Current status of civil society: a synthesis

Iranian civil society grew considerably under the 8-year presidency of Khatami. However, since 2005, as a result of the dominance of anti-civil society discourse in Iranian politics and society, Iranian civil society has faced new threats and constraints.

Ahmadinezhad won the 2005 presidential election by embracing the populist promises of the Khomeini era, namely justice and well-being for the poor. His promises mobilized the poor who felt neglected and left behind. In his campaign broadcast on television, the cameras showed his home with a modest sitting room, furnished with an inexpensive carpet and large cushions placed against the walls (Naji 2008: 70). He stressed the importance of national security, and promised to raise wages and salaries, and to deal with poverty and unemployment.

Moreover, he had the support of almost all hardliners and hundreds of thousands of members of *Basij* and the Revolutionary Guard (Naji 2008: 71). At the same time the reformers were divided, and some segments of society were disappointed by the reformists' unfulfilled promises. Many boycotted the election and this paved the way for Ahmadinezhad to win the election (see Naji 2008).

Since 2005, Iranian civil society has undergone a transformation. The outcome of the 2005 presidential election has profoundly affected the activities of civil society. The political group that won the election favors populist economic policies, politics, and ideological discourse. Ahmadinezhad's victory brought to power a completely new set of people whose extreme views had previously kept them away from key positions (Naji 2008: xii).

The policies of the new government have weakened Iranian civil society since 2005. Some CSOs have suspended their operations, and others have reduced their activities. Some have tried to adapt to the new conditions, and others have been prevented from working by the government. However, some organizations have continued to work unabated, in spite of political repression.

Ahmadinezhad's government considers civil society a Trojan horse, and a US-sponsored project for velvet revolutions. Moreover, it considers Iranian civil society as an ally of pro-reform groups and the opposition. The reason for this view is that Iranian civil society is the only space in which pro-reform and counterhegemonic ideas can be expressed. In other words, it is the only place in which the voices of marginalized groups can be heard. Therefore, the policy of the government since 2005 has been to regulate the territory of the Iranian civil society, i.e. the universities, the press, voluntary organizations, etc. Ahmadinezhad's government denounces civil society and democracy, and considers it to be an evil force, a Western phenomenon, a means of opposing Islam, and a source of immorality and perversity. Also, because of its populist approach, civil society is to be considered an intruder on the populist system (Razzaghi 2007). Ahmadinezhad's government has implemented many policies that limit Iranian civil society in order to preempt a so-called velvet revolution in the country. Political freedom has been restricted, and civil society activists are routinely accused of "action against national security," "propaganda against the system," or spying on behalf of the USA or other Western countries (Razzaghi 2007).

Ahmadinezhad's government has aggressively undermined CSOs since 2005 by rejecting their applications for registration, toughening existing laws and regulations that pertain to the CSOs, eliminating subsidies, spreading fear and terror among civil society activists, destroying the relationship between Iranian CSOs and their international counterparts, intervening in the affairs of the CSOs and their networks, and suppressing and restricting the activities of civil society activists, etc. (Razzaghi 2007).

Despite the glacial pace of reform and restriction of civil society activities during Ahmadinezhad's presidency, the willingness of people for change and reform is so strong and varied that it has not been hindered.

Khatami's political career may have come to an end by the 2005 presidential election, but the movement he inspired during his presidency is now integrated into the everyday life of Iranian politics. The remarkable events surrounding the 2009 Iranian election, which astonished the world, are clear examples of this claim.

Towards a strong civil society: tensions and contradictions

Despite the rapid development of civil society discourse, Iranian civil society is still struggling to become a strong civil society (see Chapter 5). However, the challenges to civil society in the Iranian case are directly related to the challenges facing Iranian society, politics, and economy (Razzaghi 2007).

The development patterns of the political system and the state–society relationship during the last century, are probably the most important factors in understanding the nature and challenges faced by civil society in the Iranian context.

Except for some very short periods, the nature of the state in Iran has always been authoritarian, and there has always been a conflict between the state and society. Under the Islamic republic this conflict intensified, and the hegemonic state began to exert control and interfere in all areas of peoples' lives. It dominated all existing space, leaving no space for civil society.

However, for a civil society to function properly, different groups and ideologies must coexist. If a government aims to homogenize these groups, civil society fails to perform its role of mediating power relations. The greatest obstacle to civil society during Khatami's presidency was that after two decades of dominance of the so-called conservative discourse in which the revolution and values from the war such as fundamentalism, anti-Westernization, and martyrdom were advocated and practiced, religious institutions and most governmental institutions were not willing to allow their power to be mediated through civil institutions. Consequently, the conservative front was opposing the movement and there was still a lack of balance in the power relations between independent institutions and the government (Jalaipur 2003).

In addition, the president, who served as the head of the reform movement, has limited powers within the Iranian constitution. Although the president is the highest elected official in the Islamic Republic of Iran, he is second to the Supreme Leader, who is not elected by people, but by the Assembly of Experts (*Majlis-e Khobregan*). The Assembly of Experts is a body of 86 Islamic scholars, which is responsible for electing and removing the Supreme Leader. The president does not have full control over foreign policy or the armed forces, which are under the control of the Supreme Leader. Moreover, the Guardian Council ensures that legislation passed by parliament is compatible with the criteria of Islam and constitution. In other words, they have the power to veto laws passed by parliament. Thus, the Supreme Leader and the Guardian Council play the most important roles in the politics of the Islamic Republic. As both are proponents of conservative ideology, they have actively resisted calls to change the structure of the government.

As Halliday (2007: xiv) argues, "much of the history of modern Iran, has involved a tension between challenging indigenous authoritarian power by invoking international standards, of rights, constitutional governments and accountability and at the same time challenging the influence of external powers in the name of Iranian independence and values." Furthermore, the impact of globalization on the Iranian state and society has been contradictory. In contemporary Iran, on the one hand, there is an attempt to challenge many Iranian laws and practices by invoking international principles. On the other hand, globalization has mostly been considered antagonistic to Islamic values. Moreover, whenever the conservatives face a threat to their power, they employ "conspiracy theory" rhetoric, and warn of "cultural imperialism" (Jalaipur 2003).

Khatami's policies provoked the ire of many hardliners. In October 1998, they rejected the applications of over 200 of the 396 clerics who registered as candidates for the Assembly of Experts. In late 1998, there was a case of serial murders of Iranian intellectuals, known as the "Chain Murders of Iran." All those who were murdered or disappeared were Iranians who had been critical of the Islamic Republic.

Throughout 1998 and 1999, there was a campaign carried out against the reform movement from the conservative segment of the state. Many reformists, even clerical reformists, were summoned for questioning or were prosecuted for different reasons. Many reformist newspapers and journals were forced to close. In the summer of 1999, following a student demonstration at the University of Tehran against the closure of pro-Khatami newspapers, members of the *Ansar-e Hizbollah*, a militant conservative Islamic group in Iran, attacked the student dormitory at night and beat up the students. Thousands of students and protesters took to the streets of Tehran. The protest turned into a violent street riot, spreading to some other cities and lasting 6 days. In March 2000, Saeed Hajjarian, the main theorist of Khatami's reforms, survived an assassination attempt but sustained injuries that left him paralyzed for life. In April 2000, 12 newspapers and six magazines with more than one million readers were closed down. In June 2002, Hashem Aghajari, a university professor, and a critic of the Islamic republic, gave an address to commemorate the 25th anniversary of the death of Dr. Ali Shariati, in which he criticized some of the existing Islamic practices in Iran for being in contradiction with the original practices and ideology of Islam. He called for "Islamic Protestantism" and reform in Islam. He was arrested shortly thereafter and sentenced to death. The announcement of the death sentence provoked a massive student protest in Tehran and other cities.

As a consequence of these incidents, people became disappointed by the slow pace of change during Khatami's first term, and they demanded more autonomy for civil society. This led many who voted for him in the first term of his presidency to boycott the second election, and for many activists to suspend their activities.

Conclusion

Despite political and social upheavals, a new discourse has become dominant in Iran since 1997, which is the discourse of civil society and public sphere. Moreover, the earlier call for civil society has been replaced with new discourses, narratives, and forms of resistance in Iran. This indicates that Iranian society has undergone deep social changes. However, these changes are reflected not only in the emergence of new discourses, narratives, and forms of resistance, but also in the development of a middle class, which is highly educated.

The population grew dramatically and urbanization boomed after the 1979 revolution. Moreover, the increase in the number of primary schools, high schools, universities, and other providers of higher education in the country, led to increased public social awareness (this led particularly to the empowerment of women within the middle class). A new generation of social activists has emerged in Iran, which has new demands, ideologies, identities, and worldviews. As Khosrokhavar describes, "they amount to a large social movement with modern features that distinguish it from the past." Being open to the globalized world, this new generation of social activists promotes a new culture and literature for civil society, democracy, citizenship, and human rights in Iranian society (as was explained in Chapter 2, the fundamental changes have become even more obvious since the June 2009 uprising).

Furthermore, the emergence of the information-society has changed and influenced all kinds of individual and social actions. This development, in all aspects of life, has provided activists with an opportunity to use new resources and methods to promote their ideas in a more effective way. The extensive use of the internet as a mobilizing tool and a platform in the uprisings of June 2009 (see Chapter 2) is an obvious example of the structural changes that have occurred in the sphere of media and information. These structural changes are affecting future events and developments in Iranian society.

4 From a movement for civil society towards a movement for the environment

Introduction

The environmental movement in Iran is a social movement, which operates as a force for change. It calls not only for reform and alteration of the relationship between nature and humans, but also between government and citizens. Environmentalists' acts are purposive collective actions with clear objectives.

This chapter is intended to establish that collective action around environmental concerns is not fragmented social action but can be categorized as a social movement. Furthermore, an understanding of how and why this social phenomenon has emerged in Iran is provided. Third, characteristics of the Iranian environmental movement in Tehran (as the core of the movement) and Rasht (as a peripheral example) are explained. Environmental groups in these two cities are described and compared in terms of their main focus. Moreover, the structure of the movement in terms of goals, activities, and participants, and an analysis of its challenges and current status also are examined. The aim is not to introduce all environmental groups, but to provide a guide for better understanding of them.

Environmentalism: emergence of a social movement in Iran?

As was explained in Chapter 1, a social movement is a system of a collective actions by a group of people who are consciously aiming to make, or resisting, a specific change. They have a higher level of organization than mobs or crowds, but less than formal and bureaucratic organizations. In order to define collective action as a social movement, we need to make reference to three basic features: shared goals (aiming to make a social change, but not for political power), loose organizational structure, and systematic collectivity.

According to observations, and with reference to interviews, environmental groups in Iran have been consciously mobilizing themselves and their resources in order to bring about social change. Their ultimate goal has been to introduce at least two different levels of change: firstly, many environmental organizations have focused their activity on consciousness raising and educational campaigns by organizing seminars, exhibitions, conferences, festivals, trips, publications, etc. Through these actions, new values, attitudes, and lifestyles have been introduced. Moreover, citizens have been encouraged to be active participants of civic affairs. Secondly, by criticizing governmental attitudes towards the environment, and through campaigns, demonstrations, and lobbying, they actively challenge the state and its inefficient institutions.

Moreover, environmental groups all follow a basic level of organization, although membership rules and structure are very flexible. Individuals can join and leave easily without any strong pressure. In most cases, submitting a membership form and paying membership dues are the only prerequisites. However, for some members this is their only activity, as they never take part in any other action. There is usually a very small number of people who act as permanent participants of the non-governmental organization (NGO); others just participate in specific events. Moreover, there is rarely a strict hierarchy in organizational structure. Participatory interaction is dominant in many groups.

Although they vary in their interests, forms of action, and level of activities, environmental groups are not just fragmented groups concerned about the environment. There is a level of cooperation and collectivity between them. Although a few environmental groups are organized around single issues such as water conservation or environmental law, most are concerned with more general issues. Broadly speaking, the relationship between humans and nature is central to their concerns. It is common for a few groups to organize an event together or work on the same project, and their collaboration is most evident during symbolic events such as The Day of the Clean Air or The Mountain Day. During environmental festivals and seminars a huge number of environmental groups gather and work together. Furthermore, during protests and campaigns against a particularly controversial environmental policy (i.e. for preventing an environmentally harmful action), they exhibit a high level of cooperation. Additionally, there are some links between locally based NGOs and national and international organizations. The NGOs are connected with the Iranian Department of Environment, municipalities, and the Forests, Range and Watershed Management Organization of Iran, which are the most important national environmental organizations. These connections include participation in joint projects and collaborative educational workshops and seminars. Among the international organizations, UNDP (United Nations Development Programs) and GEF (Global Environment Facility) are the partners of many environmental NGOs in Iran (in Iran, the branches of UNDP and GEF are the most common international organizations with which to work).[1] The weak connection between Iranian and foreign organizations indicates that the movement does not identify itself with the international environmental community. Instead, environmental groups remain firmly embedded in Iranian society, with some following the slogan of "think globally act locally."

Above all, there are networks of organizations at regional and national levels, within which many NGOs meet to communicate and lobby. These networks facilitate cooperation, collective action, networking, and sharing of information between environmental groups. As some of the activists declare:

> When we started the network, most of the NGOs were mostly active in symbolic actions and general issues. We wanted to make a platform for them to become specialized and professionalized. Moreover, we wished to create a stage for international connections.

or:

> Although empowering of the environmental nongovernmental organizations was one of our goals, our main aim was to solve the legal problems of authorizing our work. At that time the officials even didn't know what a NGO is. So we decided to bring all the environmental NGOs to lead a campaign for easier authorization.

or:

> We came to the idea of establishing the network because; the international organizations wanted to work with us, but they needed a centrality. They required a stage where, all the NGOs could meet. In this way they could contact us easier.

Within these environmental networks, different groups from all over the country gather to share information and discuss problems a few times per year. As the head of the National Environment Network states: "Our main goal is to link the activities of all environmental groups together and make the 'environment' a priority for the government, families and individuals."

From the discussion above, it is clear that environmental activism in Iran is not just spontaneous fragmented social action. To reiterate, environmental groups share three common features: shared goals in bringing societal change, a loose level of organization, and systematic collectivity. Thus, it is clear that a social movement has emerged around environmental issues in Iran.

Why has a social movement emerged around environmental issues?

Why has the environment become an issue around which individuals have mobilized in recent years in Iranian society? If it was simply because of environmental disasters occurring within the country, it should have started years ago. Therefore, in addition to environmental degradation, a profound change has occurred in how Iranians perceive the relationship between humans and nature, and their relationship with the state. Society has gone through structural transformations that have made people think and act differently.

Iran's environmental movement emerged within a different social context from that of the West. In most developed societies, recognition of environmental damage caused by industrialization began in the 1970s (Pickvance 1998: 73). However, Iran did not experience a comparable exhaustion of its natural resources through over-consumption. Nevertheless, the most educated sections of Iranian society embraced the green ideologies of the West in the 1980s. However, until the early 1990s, almost any kind of organized civic activity was impossible and not tolerated by the state.

The environmental movement in Iran began to develop in the 1990s, although it is difficult to pinpoint an exact date. As a consequence of weak governmental organizations during the years after the revolution, explosive population growth, urbanization, and industrial mismanagement, as well as the devastation brought on by 8 years of war with Iraq, resulted in numerous environmental problems such as air pollution, water and soil contamination, and destruction and over-exploitation of natural resources. Environmental groups sprang up in the early 1990s, and had peaked by the late 1990s and early 2000s. Their evolution has been directly linked to the emergence of the reform movement, and relaxation of existing legal constraints (although there was small group mobilization concerning environmental issues at earlier stages in

Iranian history, it was in the late 1990s and especially 1997–2000 when environmentalism started to gain momentum as a social movement).

Claus Offe (1987) emphasizes political exclusion as an important factor for individuals joining social movements. The oppressive years after the Islamic revolution, and the 8-year war, which contributed to an even more restricted political atmosphere in Iran, meant the majority of people felt excluded from decision making processes. In the aftermath of the 1997 presidential election, and with the emergence of a movement for reform and civil society, individuals were exposed to the ideas of public participation and citizenship rights (see Chapter 3). Phrases such as "willingness to be an active member of society," "participation in public life," "doing something for the nation," etc., were often given as some of the main motivations for establishing an environmental group among interviewees.

Furthermore, restructuring of the Iranian Department of Environment in 1997 led to the launch of an action called the National Action Plan for Environmental Protection, which was a call for collaboration between related official organizations and civil society. A committee on the issue of public participation was organized, and it was mainly concentrated on implementation of different programs to unite various groups of people, associations, factories, etc., around environmental issues (*Barnameh-ye azm-e melli baraye hefazat az mohit-e zist* 1999). Moreover, in 1998, the Public Participation Bureau was founded within the Iranian Department of Environment. Its aim was to assist environmental NGOs.

Masumeh Ebtekar became the first female vice president and the head of Iranian Department of Environment during Khatami's administration, and she played a significant role in shaping and encouraging environmental activism. Under her administration, the Iranian Department of Environment was reorganized and gained international recognition. In 2006, the United Nations Environment Programme (UNEP) named Ebtekar as one of seven Champions of the Earth (an international environmental award, which goes to environmental leaders who have exemplified inspiration, leadership, action, and innovation).

In the 1980s and early 1990s, environmental concerns became some of the most important issues in Western countries. In the 1990s, environmentalism started to become a global issue. Global warming, problems with the ozone layer, the destruction of tropical rain forests, and other issues attracted the attention of many people around the world. The 1992 United Nations Conference on global environmental issues—known as the Rio Summit—was a clear symbol of these new concerns. More than 120 nations, including Iran, as well as numerous environmental groups, participated in the summit. One of the main focuses of the conference was to encourage participation in environmental NGOs.

Three years later, in Beijing, the Women's Conference of 1995 highlighted environmentalism, women, and the relationship between the two as fundamental issues. This accelerated creation of a scientific and educational context for the environment. It provided the necessary information for sensitizing citizens and officials to the importance of growing environmental problems. Since then, there has been a growing concern about environmental issues in Iran. One activist notes:

> Although a few environmental NGOS were active before Khatami's election, environmentalism started to operate as a social movement under his presidency. Following the Stockholm conference on the environment, and other international actions about the environment, the Department of Environment in Iran was restructured and became compatible with the new development plans. Furthermore, in the universities topics on environment and relevant issues started to gain importance. Above all, The Rio Summit played a major role in consciousness raising about global environmental problems. However, before Khatami the environmental concerns were mostly scientific whereas, in late 1990s they were transferred to a social movement and functioned through civil society organizations.

Many environmental activists are Western-educated, and were exposed to environmentalism during their years spent in Europe and the USA. Some participated in environmental movements in these countries. After returning to Iran, they sought to implement their knowledge by establishing environmental groups.

The role of the media in bringing environmental issues to public attention is undeniable. As Manuel Castells (2004) has argued, the constant presence of environmental issues in the media has not only led to legitimization of green values but also has contributed to the construction of a specific identity. Although controlling the media has been one of the most important goals of the Islamic republic from the very beginning, the dynamics of the 1990s were different from those of previous years (Mohammadi 2006). Technological changes in modes of message delivery, specifically satellite television and the internet, have played an important role in raising and shaping environmental awareness and activity in Iran. Many groups advised that national media, such as radio, television, and the press, had become the main channel for environmental education. From the late 1990s to the present, there have been a number of articles and reports on the environment in newspapers. Many campaigns, projects, and demonstrations became possible only through the use of such media for spreading information. A few groups even participated in joint programs with radio and television.

Another important factor in stimulating environmental activism was the 2001 launch of the Global Environment Facility (GEF) funded Small Grants Program (SGP). The SGP supports activities of NGOs and community-based organizations (CBOs) in developing countries towards the mitigation of climate change, conservation of biodiversity, protection of international waters, reduction of the impact of persistent organic pollutants, and prevention of land degradation while generating sustainable livelihoods. The SGP is implemented by the United Nations Development Program.

In Iran, the SGP has produced a supportive environment for cooperation between CBOs, civil society organizations (CSOs), the government and United Nations organizations on issues related to GEF areas of concern. Many environmental NGOs in Iran have been partners of different projects implemented by the GEF. Availability of funding for environmental projects has significantly influenced the stimulation of environmentalism in Iran.

In the early 1990s very few environmental groups existed in Iran. However, the most prominent were the Green Front of Iran, the Women's Society for the Campaign against Environmental Pollution, and the Mountain Environmental Protection Association.

The Green Front of Iran was founded by four medical students in Tehran in 1989, and received authorization in 1994. The first and primary goal of the Green Front of Iran was to raise public awareness on environmental issues, and it implemented several programs to this end. Its tactics were a combination of confronting authorities on different issues, and organizing events with the intention of raising public interest. The Green Front of Iran was the most popular environmental group with more than 5,000 members across the country by the beginning of 2007, when the group faced structural changes in its organizational level and membership.

The Women's Society for the Campaign against Environmental Pollution is another example of an early environmental NGO. It was established in 1992, and was registered in 1994. Mahlaqa Mallah, the founder of the group who is known as "the mother of Iran's environment" was educated in France, and her main concern over the years has been the environment and the role of women in the life-cycle. Her eco-feminist ideology has made her conclude that any step towards environmentalism should include and address the role of women in society. Since the early 1990s the main focuses of the Women's Society for the Campaign against Environmental Pollution have been consciousness raising and confronting the government with environmental issues. With many branches throughout the country, the Women's Society for the Campaign against Environmental Pollution is today, following the structural changes of the Green Front of Iran, the largest environmental group in Iran.

The Mountain Environmental Protection Association focused on the single issue of "mountain protection" in 1989, and was officially registered in 1997. As the founder claims:

> We were just a group of people interested in the mountains. However, some of us were political activists of the revolution years. When we started to work together we even didn't know what a NGO is. We just felt that the mountains were in danger of serious destruction, so we decided to protect them. But for some years we just worked without registering our group.

During the period 1997–2005, the number of environmental groups increased dramatically. According to data provided by the Iranian Department of the Environment, during this period 640 environmental NGOs were formed all over the country.

Today, cultural issues are at the center of environmental activities. Moreover, environmentalists are engaged in issues that influence and promote environmental change. Organizing campaigns and protests, and lobbying officials are their other main activities. These organizations differ in size, locality, strategy, and activities.

Environmentalism in action

European history of environmentalism has two distinct periods of environmental mobilization. The first phase, at the beginning of the twentieth century, focused public attention and organizational efforts on issues of wildlife protection and the preservation of national cultural and natural treasures. At this stage, environmentalists were concerned with maintenance of species, protection of habitats, and preservation of the nation's heritage (Dalton 1994).

The second phase started in the 1960s and 1970s. This phase addressed new environmental problems and quality of life concerns,

and had a new ecological orientation. Also, environmentalists demanded fundamental social changes while addressing new environmental
problems of advanced industrial societies, such as nuclear power, industrial pollution, acid rain, etc. The activists of the first phase accepted
the existing sociopolitical order, pursuing their goals within existing
socioeconomic structures. In the second phase of environmentalism,
basic changes in social and political relations were viewed as prerequisites for addressing environmental problems. Activists looked
for a new societal model as a solution to environmental problems
(Dalton 1994).

In Iran, these two streams of environmentalism emerged simultaneously, being represented within different organizations. As there is no
single understanding of environmentalism and it has different con-
ceptualizations, environmentalists are concerned with many different
issues. However, "protection of nature" and "improvement of the
quality of life" are among the most common issues raised by almost all
groups.

Center of the movement: Tehran

Within the multiplicity of the environmental movement in Tehran, we
can discern eight major strands from the main focus, according to the
issues around which the groups were launched. This does not mean
that the groups are exclusively concerned with these issues, but the
categorization highlights their focus.

- Climate change-pollution
- Research-scientific
- Women-environment
- Youth-environment
- Wildlife
- Single issue
- General issue
- Virtual environmentalism

1. Climate change-pollution

Activists of this strand are professional athletes, with numbers ranging
from 100 to 2,000; however, a core of 50–200 members remain permanently active. There are two different kinds of environmental groups
within this strand. One group of NGOs is concerned only with mountains, and issues related to mountain conservation. As Tehran is

located at the foot of the Alborz Mountain Range, the people of Tehran and its suburbs have a close connection to the mountains. Many people, especially the younger generation, spend holidays and weekends in the mountains surrounding Tehran. Moreover, mountains have a special place in Persian mythology and folklore, and have always been symbols of Iranian resistance against despotism in Persian literature. Thus, they are important features of Iranian life, especially for the people living in close proximity to them. In recent years, vegetation and wildlife in the mountains have experienced extreme changes, arousing the concern of many environmentalists. According to one activist:

> When we started our work, only a few NGOs existed, and they were not involving people in their actions. Their activities were rather limited. That is why we decided to start the first move! Our first action was removing the garbage from the mountains. Later on we started planting trees. In the beginning we were alone but later other groups joined us too. Our third campaign became a huge act which attracted the officials as well. Finally, the officials started to realize the problems of the mountains surrounding Tehran. We felt successful because the first noise we made brought some people together. Moreover, the officials started to wake up and realize the danger that was threatening our environment.

Another leader emphasizes the importance of syndicates to support the issues related to the mountains. He explains: "As in Iran there is no such syndicates, we decided to establish a NGO to support the people, who are concerned with mountains."

The second group within this strand consists of a NGO focused only on promoting bicycle riding. The founder of the *Anjoman-e Docharkheh Savari-e Parvaneh-ye Sabz* (Green Papillon) is a professional cyclist who has deep concerns for the environment. His main goal in starting this environmental group has been to raise awareness on the issues of pollution control, climate change, and the greenhouse effect. As the leader of the group points out:

> Using a bicycle as a means of transportation is totally new for Iranians. That is why it attracts a lot of people. Especially women join our group very eagerly because they were never allowed to do sports in public, and this gives them opportunity to be out and experience something new. Almost everyone joins because they find cycling a relaxing sport. Many of our members are not

concerned about the environment in the beginning, when they join our group. They only want to make some changes in their lives. But when they start working with us, they receive environmental training and they start getting interested in environmental issues such as pollution control and climate change. They enjoy the idea of being exposed to new perspectives concerned with their everyday lives.

Activists from this strand of environmentalism mainly engage in symbolic actions, release publications, campaign, and lobby officials. Moreover, they hold seminars, workshops, and meetings on relevant issues. Finally, they work in joint projects with some governmental bodies.

2. Research-scientific

Compared with the other strands, this strand includes a huge number of NGOs. The activists of this group are all professionals (professors, experts, graduate students) from different fields of environmental sciences to human sciences. Due to the lack of knowledge about environmental issues among the public and officials, activists in this group are concerned with consciousness raising. Groups typically have small membership, varying from 10 to 20 members, because they are not concerned with mobilization on a large scale.

Except for one group that limits its activity to purely scientific work, the NGOs all join symbolic actions, protests, and campaigns. Thus, although activists within this strand are concentrated on scientific issues, their activities go beyond pure research. A representative of the group that prefers to avoid any protest or campaign states that:

> We are scientific, not social, not economic, and not cultural!!! We have always had problems with other environmental NGOs because they wanted us to follow them and we had our own way. They were telling us we are making mistake in not being political. They wanted us to participate in their campaigns, demonstrations and protests. But we wanted to do more scientific work. At some point we were excluded from all other groups and most of the environmental groups didn't care about our work anymore.

Groups of this strand are mostly busy with consciousness raising through scientific publications and workshops, and, on occasion, campaigns and protests. They also take part in joint projects with some official organizations. Usually, the groups do not have any specialization; however, there is one NGO that focuses only on Environmental Law. The founders of *Hoghugh-e Mohit-e Zist* (Environmental Law) are among the leaders of a national campaign to force the government to apply a law for NGOs. An activist from this group told us:

> In the late 1990s, after mushrooming of so many NGOs, they were facing an obvious problem, which was an absence of law to protect the NGO and its activities. As NGOs were previously unknown in Iran, their essence was a mystery for the government and officials. In the beginning their activities fell under the law for political parties, but in fact there is a huge difference between NGOs and political parties. An NGO is a non-political organization, whereas political party is entirely political. Activists launched a campaign to negotiate the possibility of passing a law for NGOs. However, after many years there is still no specific law which supports NGOs. In our own NGO our aim is to bring up the issue of the environment and necessity of laws to support environmental issues.

3. Women-environment

In general, these organizations believe in the important role of women in environmental issues. Two significant assumptions are held by these groups: first, they are conscious of the historical role of women in environmental conservation. Second, they are aware of the importance of women's empowerment in a society in which women have always been suppressed. As one activist says:

> My mother had an important impact on me. She was not an educated woman, but a very special woman in her time. She fought against many patriarchal structures of society during her life. It was because of her that I started to stand up for my own rights, and the improvement of women's status. My personal interests for nature and environment, being confronted with women issues, gave me the idea of establishing an NGO, which brings together the 'women' and the 'environment'. Before the revolution I started to think about establishing such a NGO but then, the revolution and the war period made that impossible. I waited many years to establish this NGO.

Most of the leaders and activists of these groups are women. Although most are educated women, housewives and lesser educated middle class women, and the lower class are the target of many activities and projects. Through publications, seminars, workshops, and lobbying officials, they foster environmental knowledge and contribute to the task of consciousness raising.

There is an evident difference in the size of the two organizations studied in this strand. Whereas one, *Jamiat-e Zanan-e Mobarez ba Aludegi-e Mohit-e Zist* (the Women's Society for the Campaign against Environmental Pollution), has been able to mobilize thousands of people in Tehran and other cities (through different branches), the other, *Anjoman-e Zanan-e Irani-e Tarafdar-e Toseh-ye Paidar-e Mohit-e Zist* (Society of Iranian Women for Sustainable Development), is rather limited in its membership (around 100 members).

4. Youth-environment

These NGOs concentrate on the issues of environment and youth. Authorized by the Youth National Organization[2] within the period 1997–2003, they all received strong support when initially founded. Their leaders and members are all young people aged from 16 to 35, who are interested in sociopolitical participation by way of collective action. Through interviews, it became clear that the activists of this strand are not actually particularly concerned with the environment. Instead, as environmental activity is not very controversial and still tolerated to some degree by officials, they have chosen to frame themselves as "environmentalists" in order to bring young people into the sociopolitical sphere. Their activities are mainly holding workshops and seminars for youth, engaging in research and distributing publications, scientific trips, street shows, demonstrations, exhibitions, and, in some cases, participation in joint projects with municipalities. The number of activists in the smallest organization of this type is 50, whereas the largest has approximately 1,000 members.

However, following the presidential election of 2005 and a decline in state support of the Youth National Organization, there has been a dramatic downturn in the activities of many of these groups.

5. Wildlife

Issues related to wildlife have usually been a source of conflict between environmentalists, hunters, and the government. Hunters and many local people have historically viewed animals as food, and the source of their livelihood. Some animals like bears, wolves, snakes, etc., are considered dangerous. Some, such as dogs, are considered dirty (*najes*) according to Islamic principles. The activists of this strand oppose any kind of animal cruelty. Preserving the ecosystem and its species is their main goal. They focus mostly on endangered species such as the Persian cheetah, relationships between animals and humans, and the laws that regulate these relationships.

The oldest group of this strand, *Anjoman-e Hemayat az Heyvanat* (the Iranian Society for the Prevention of Cruelty to Animals), started by promoting a culture of animal rights. The leader of the group, who is a professor of veterinary medicine, explains:

> While working at the university clinic with animals, I realized that there are people who collect injured animals from the streets, and bring them to the university clinic. Observing this, I came to the idea of establishing a NGO where all the people who care for animals can gather and share ideas. Furthermore, I thought through a collective act we could change the dominant culture, and be more effective.

Members are mostly young people seeking a way into public life, whereas some are exclusively interested in animal issues. This group has attracted around 3,500 members and has a few branches in other cities. Its work is mostly concentrated on an educational level, working with small children and youth. The main activity is holding classes and workshops in kindergartens and schools, but the group also participates in symbolic actions, organizes educational tours and trips, and holds exhibitions and street shows. Furthermore, it lobbies officials in an attempt to secure animal-friendly legislation (especially for dogs, which are considered dirty and untouchable (*najes*) according to Islam).

Anjoman-e Yuzpalang-e Irani (the Iranian Cheetah Society) is primarily concerned with the Asiatic cheetah in Iran. Its primary goals have been research into and consciousness raising about the Asiatic cheetah and its endangered status. However, after several years of work and investigation, the group realized that it is not only the habitat of the cheetah that is threatened by development, but those of all large carnivores. Today, group activities have expanded to research and community education on issues concerning all large carnivores and the relation to human beings. Moreover, it empowers local NGOs on the issue, in order to make them work effectively in their own regions. There are around 350 activists in this group, mostly young people who are interested in environment and wildlife.

6. Single issue

The sixth strand of the movement consists of groups that focus only on one specific issue. For example, *Goruh-e Bacheh-ha-ye Ab* (Water Kids Group) is concerned only with water and water-related issues. As Iran is a dry land, availability of water has always been a source of concern. As the founder of the NGO claims:

> Industrialization has caused a lot of problems concerning clean water. Moreover, Iran being a dry land has always faced water problems be it for agricultural use or everyday life. In order to achieve to some standards we need to educate the people. Some social structures should change, in order to enable us solve our problems. Above all, structural changes in our political system are necessary. Absence of a strong civil society causes a lot of problems for social movements and that is why consciousness raising is our main objective.

The founders were a group of environmental activists within the Center for Dialog Among Civilizations.[3] After a few years they decided to establish an NGO to pursue their goals through workshops and seminars, publication of books and CDs, and participation in joint projects with related official organizations, etc. *Goruh-e Bacheh-ha-ye Ab* emphasizes the important role of water in the life cycle. It has about 50 active members from different sections of society, but mostly the younger generation. What makes this group different from other groups is that there is no inactive system of membership. Participants are considered members only if they actively participate in group activities. Therefore, unlike others, the group does not have an open, loose structure.

Mosseseh-ye Toseh-ye Rusta-ye Sabz (Institute of Green Rural Development) is concentrated only on issues related to agriculture. Its main aims are to work against the widespread use of pesticides and to promote organic agriculture. The founder of the NGO notes that:

> My husband and I both have studied in the fields of environment and rural development. In the beginning we were working with the government but within the governmental framework it was not possible for us to implement our new ideas. We were very restricted. So we decided to establish a NGO where we could enjoy a relative freedom.

As pioneer of the Farmers' Field School in Iran, the group's main concern is rural development. The Farmers' Field School has developed an empowerment course for peasants. Members of the NGO teach peasants how to control their product in the farm, and promote organic and other sustainable methods of farming. Following attendance on the course, the peasants can educate other peasants, with the aim being continuous farmer education.

Moreover, *Mo'sesseh-ye Tose'h-ye Rusta-ye Sabz* has founded a network through which it distributes the peasants' organic products directly to consumers. Unlike in European countries, there are not many places providing Iranian consumers with organic products. Therefore, such distribution networks are a great support to peasants attempting to grow and market organic produce. Membership of the group remains rather limited; members are generally people with backgrounds in rural development or environmental studies.

7. General issue

The environmental groups of this strand usually do not focus on any specific issue, rather they are concerned with environmental issues in general.

Jebheh-ye Sabz-e Iran (the Green Front of Iran) is the oldest group within this strand of NGOs. Its aim is to raise public awareness on environmental issues all over the country. It is heavily influenced by the ideology and activities of Greenpeace; activists consider implementing activities like those of Greenpeace (there is no branch of Greenpeace in Iran). Key activities have been symbolic actions, such as planting trees, taking part in demonstrations and campaigns, and holding seminars and meetings. Consciousness raising and community empowerment are the main objectives.

In 2007, membership had reached 5,000, with considerable numbers of branches in different cities. Members come from different backgrounds and age groups of the middle class. However, since 2007 the group has faced internal problems, which led to some structural changes.

Anjoman-e Javanan-e Hafez-e Zamin (the Society for Young Protectors of the Earth) was established by five students of natural resources.

> In the university classes we used to hear about a lot of environmental problems. Most of the time the professors used to say that we cannot do anything about the problems. They always proposed

odd and strange solutions. So, we decided to start a group in order to bring some changes. In the beginning we were only five, but after a short period of time many other people joined our NGO.

Originally, the primary goal was to foster public awareness, but subsequently they activities were redirected towards more professional work such as participating in SGP (the GEF small Grants Program). The first phase of activity consisted of symbolic actions, and participation in protests and campaigns. For example, a recycling project was implemented in one district of Tehran and workshop were held to encourage people to recycle. The number of members was reduced from 400 to 40, who were active in the SGP project at the time of conducting the interview in the summer of 2007. The majority of the activists are youth, university students, and recent graduates.

8. Virtual environmentalism

The internet has become a primary tool for environmentalists in the campaign to foster public awareness. During the past 10 years use of the internet has significantly grown in Iran. Faced with censorship in other media, the internet provides a space where individuals can publish their ideas without the fear of reprisal. The most common use of the internet in this respect has been personal weblogs. These websites are a site for open debates, discussions, and consciousness raising.

An example of the periphery: Rasht

Only one major strand of environmental groups is present in Rasht. Astonishingly, all groups are concentrated on nature conservation, although there are differences between the groups. Conservationism is not the only concern. The groups aim to foster changes in life style and are critical of the state.

Rasht is in the center of Gilan province. It is one of the most forested and green provinces of Iran and lies along the Caspian Sea. The livelihoods of many people in this area are dependent on the sea, and the humid climate of the region has made agriculture, especially rice cultivation, a main activity. Moreover, although during the warm seasons the climate is quite humid, the cool and pleasant coastline attract thousands of tourists who come to the seashore and forests. This is another reason why the forests and the Caspian Sea are the two of the most important natural features for people in the province. "Many

people in Gilan are connected to the sea or the forest for their livelihoods. So, an environmental NGO in this region should also do
something which, is related to the concerns of the people in this
region," commented the leader of one of the groups.

As a consequence of environmentally destructive policies and the
rapid growth of tourism in the region in recent years, environmental
degradation (especially water pollution and deforestation) has been
enormous. Therefore, for the people of Gilan, environmental issues
have become livelihood issues, connected to their everyday lives. Furthermore, the massive amount of garbage in the region, and extreme
levels of sea and river pollution have severely impacted the health of
the local population. Many of the environmental groups, therefore,
concentrate their work on forest and sea conservation.

Activities of environmental groups in Rasht focus on two main
issues: first, consciousness raising through seminars, workshops, etc.
Second, organization of campaigns to clean the beach, the forest,
and the rivers. Protests and demonstrations, in addition to lobbying
officials, are other important strategies for achieving their goals.

Although all groups are concerned with local issues (their attention
is toward nature conservation in general, be it rivers, ponds, sea, or forest),
there are NGOs that are more focused on one issue. For example,
Sepah-e Jangal (Forest Army) is concentrated only on deforestation.
Anjoman-e Kudakan-e Sabzandish (Green Minded Children Association)
believes in the importance of childhood education regarding nature
conservation, working with 3–12-year-old children in kindergartens
and primary schools.

The official numbers of members in these organizations vary from
15 to 3,000. The leaders are all from educated strata of the middle
class and hold university degrees in different fields. However, housewives make up the bulk of their memberships. There is also a large
number of unofficial activists, who participate on occasion.

Center versus periphery

Environmental groups in Rasht emerged a few years after those in
Tehran. Some environmental groups in Rasht are branches of Tehran
NGOs. A few began their work with environmental groups in Tehran,
and moved to Rasht a few years later, where they established new local
groups. However, most environmental groups in Rasht are still connected to Tehran, from whom they receive advice and guidance. This
reflects the important role of Tehran as the capital city in guiding civil
society activists.

Table 4.1 Strands of the environmental groups by focus and examples

Strands	Focus	Some examples
Climate change-pollution	Climate change Pollution control Mountain conservation	Anjoman-e Docharkheh Savari-e Parvaneh-ye Sabz (Green Papillon), Anjoman-e Hefez-e Mohit-e Kuhestan (Mountain Environmental Protection Association)
Research-scientific	Research publications	Moasseseh-ye Tahghigh va Toseh-ye Paidar-e Sarzamin (Institute of Research and Sustainable Development of Land), Anjoman-e Ofogh-e Sabzgostar (Green Hoizon Environmental Association)
Women-environment	Women empowerment Eco-feminism	Jamiat-e Zanan-e Mobarez ba Aludegi-e Mohit-e Zist (the Women's Society for the Campaign against Environmental Pollution), Anjoman-e Zanan-e Irani-e Tarafdar-e Toseh-ye Paidar-e Mohit-e Zist (Society of Iranian Women for Sustainable Development)
Youth-environment	Youth education Social justice	Tashakkol-e Hamian-e Andisheh-ye Sabz (Organization of Supporters of Green Thoughts), Tahakkol-e Shahrvandan-e Javan-e Iran (Iranian Young Citizen Organization)
Wildlife groups	Wildlife conservation	Anjoman-e Hemayat az Heyvanat (The Iranian Society for the Prevention of Cruelty to Animals), Anjoman-e Yuzpalang-e Irani (Iranian Cheetah Society)
Single issue groups	Water management Rural development	Goruh-e Bacheh-ha-ye Ab (Water Kids Group), Mosseseh-ye Toseh-ye Rusta-ye Sabz (Institute of Green Rural Development)
General issue groups	Ecological balance Conservation Public education Campaigns	Jebhe-ye Sabz-e Iran (The Green Front of Iran), Anjoman-e Javanan-e Hafez-e Zamin (The Society for Earth Young Protectors)
Virtual environmentalism	Advocacy	http://jamshidi6.blogfa.com, http://greenblog.ir/
Nature conservation	Forest conservation Sea conservation	Mosseseh-ye Sabzkaran-e Gilan (Sabzkaran Gilan), Sepah-e Jangal (Forest Army)

Unlike in Tehran, environmental NGOs in Rasht are not very diverse. They are mostly concentrated on local issues, such as conservation of the Caspian Sea and northern forests. Therefore, in contrast to environmental groups of Tehran, which in many cases have branches in other regions, the activities of the environmental NGOs in Rasht are limited to their region, and they do not engage in activities in other parts of the county. Many environmental groups in Rasht mobilized because of a precise local environmental issue, and after some time became concentrated on other issues. However, in both cities there are cases in which NGOs worked on more comprehensive issues from the beginning.

Although environmental NGOs in Tehran mushroomed in the period of 1997–2005, many were dissolved after a short time. Rasht did not experience a similar sudden increase in environmental groups, and, hence, they did not dissolve in large numbers as in Tehran.

The participants of environmental groups in both cities are mostly educated middle class people. However, except for the leaders, the body of the activists in Rasht tend to be less educated in comparison with those in Tehran. This is because Tehran, as the capital city, has a large well-educated population. In Tehran most of the leaders are middle aged, but a large proportion of young people participate in the movement because many environmental groups actively try to attract young people. As previously mentioned, one strand specifically focuses on youth. In Rasht, although the proportion of young activists is large, it is not comparable with the proportion of young activists in Tehran. In Rasht, environmental groups have attracted many middle aged activists. In both cities, the proportion of female activists in leadership and as members is high.

The organizational structure of the groups in both cities is similar. They have core activists, then members who participate in group activities on a regular basis, and then a circle of sympathizers who participate infrequently. However, the NGOs in Rasht are more hierarchically structured.

A key difference between environmental groups in Rasht and Tehran is the use of public media and internet to affect public opinion. Whereas many environmental groups in Tehran use the internet as one of their main platforms to mobilize the public, use of the internet is not popular among Rasht environmentalists.

In general, group achievements are similar in both cities. Groups both at the center and on the periphery have stopped some environmentally harmful actions (by people and officials). Moreover, as most activists claim, they have been successful in raising environmental awareness.

Limitations and challenges: struggle for survival

The environmental movement in Iran faces two sets of limitations and challenges, which can be categorized as external and internal. External challenges are direct consequences of the semi-authoritarian Iranian state. In many respects, Iranian environmentalism is a demand for political participation, and a demand for change in the political structure. As direct political activity within the framework of political parties is almost impossible within the Iranian political system, citizens look for alternative and a safer ways to claim civil and political rights. As was indicated in many interviews, "bringing some changes," "to be part of public life," "to be an active citizen," were important reasons behind the activities of many environmentalists. Many "environmental" activists use the environment as a platform for social and political change. In this case they are more "political" activists than environmentalists.

Within the current semi-authoritarian Iranian political system, environmental NGOs cannot operate autonomously. They remain in a position of interaction and negotiation with the state. As confrontational activities are not allowed, the negotiation strategy allows activists to gain maximum political and social influence. This explains why, unlike in the West, environmental activism in Iran is small-scale and organized around local issues, and, in many cases, cultural, rather than political, issues. Although environmentalism is among the most tolerated issues within the Iranian political context, activists fear that authorities will not tolerate any direct politicization, so they adhere to self-imposed censorship in order to avoid prosecution. This demonstrates the limited level of their activities. Many serious environmental problems or devastating governmental actions have attracted only weak protests, and environmentalists have been absent from others. The absence of any anti-nuclear action is an obvious example of limitations imposed on environmental activities.

Furthermore, any kind of NGO, be it environmental or not, always encounters obstacles to authorization. These problems mostly arise because the nature of NGOs is unknown to the government. Lack of a proper legal system and the absence of any law supporting NGOs, have raised many challenges. Members of an NGOs do not know how, where, and from whom they should seek authorization. Moreover, because of the absence of any concrete law, the boundaries of their activities are not clearly defined. So the activists never know how far their actions can go before the NGO is banned or they are arrested.

Authorization is a very long process—between 1 and 2 years of paperwork and bureaucracy. The long legalization process has resulted in a number of NGOs going unregistered. Although in most cases activists begin activities during the long process of registration, their activities remain limited and uncertain before registration. This creates insecurity as the government treats the activists suspiciously. Registration problems, besides the insecurities threatening the activists, are a threat to the NGO before being legally established.

There are always different approaches towards NGOs and their activities under different governments. Whereas during Khatami's presidency the civil society discourse was dominant and the NGOs were provided with different kinds of support, Ahmadinezhad's government views the NGOs as a threat to the state. After the 2005 presidential election and his victory, NGOs were ordered to restrict their activities, and activists were controlled through different channels.

Furthermore, structural changes, such as a change in the head of Iran's Department of Environment, have resulted in a serious decline in environmental policies. In early 2006 the Participation Bureau within the Department of Environment was dissolved and it became part of the Public Education Section. Consequently, all the financial and educational supports provided to environmental groups were reduced or eliminated. The withdrawal of support and policy changes towards environmentalism weakened the environmental movement. However, the wave of mobilization during the previous years and increased public attention towards environmental problems continued to facilitate further environmental actions.

The second set of limitations and challenges to the environmental movement is internal. These usually emerge as a result of opposition and personal conflicts within the groups. As the environment is considered a new issue, a general lack of environmental knowledge within the NGOs poses a serious challenge. In some cases, the undemocratic structure of some NGOs has caused serious problems within groups. As democratic discourse is a prerequisite of many kinds of social movement activities, the society should be prepared for collective democratic experience. In Iran democracy on a smaller scale, such as within the family or at school, is uncommon. Patriarchy is still the dominant discourse of social life and its institutions. Thus, although these groups mostly call for democratization through citizen participation, their internal structures remain contradictory to their stated goal.

During interviews conducted with movement activists, it became clear how the fundamental characteristics of everyday life in a non-democratic system affect ideology and activities. Leadership in some organizations is highly structured and strictly hierarchical. In one example, a very strong and active NGO exhibited an organizational structure with a low tolerance towards disagreements and new ideas, and this led to a crisis that ultimately resulted in a huge number of their members, including some key personnel, leaving the group. One activist states that:

> The leadership became old and conservative while the members were young and had new ideas. They were energetic young people who did everything for the group. But when they saw that after so many years of hard work they could never have a say in the decision-making process, they became frustrated.

In other cases, as the following two statements show, even the leaders show dissatisfaction:

> I am tired of having everything under my control. I need some break and I think new forces should come to the leadership. A few years ago, I told the members that I will leave the leadership and you choose someone instead of me. But no one accepted it.

or:

> Although in one point I decided to make a system that other members join the leadership and work together, it didn't work and I remained the only one on the leadership level. On the one hand, it was good because I had everything under my control. So, I could prevent some internal conflicts. But, on the other hand, because of my position in the group, I was the only responsible person the whole time. The socio-political problems we are facing to keep the group alive and active are many. This takes so much of my energy. Moreover, the other members don't learn the group work as there is always someone on top to lead them.

However, there have also been cases that were fully or relatively democratic. They never had a strict hierarchy, although there was always a division of labor inside the organization.

Another internal problem relates to the young population of Iran, and the huge number of young environmentalists. They have made many actions within the movement emotional not rational, from joining the movement to leaving it, and this has harmed the activities of the movement on many occasions. It has been the case that the activists tended to try and fulfill all their goals as fast as possible without giving any priority to them. As a consequence, they faced many challenges in accomplishing their goals. Furthermore, as both "environmentalism" and "civil society" are new within the Iranian context, the movement and its objectives are still not institutionalized and have not been accepted into mainstream society.

Finally, the environmental groups do not have enough sources of income available to them. Many groups are highly dependent on either governmental funding or international donors. This limits their activities, as they cannot define their projects according to the significance of environmental problems, but according to the priorities of governmental bodies or international organizations (in most cases UNDP and GEF).

General overview and analysis

A social movement starts because people are not able to fulfill their needs through already existing channels. Therefore, they seek new ways of exerting influence. That is why the development and dynamics of the environmental movements in Iran can only be understood in the context of the specific political and social conditions of Iran. Research findings indicate that the origin of the environmental movement goes back to the late 1980s, and its uprising correlates to the emergence and strengthening of the reform movement in 1997–2005. However, the initial peak of environmental group formation took place between 1998 and 2001. Since 2005, changes in the governmental policies have resulted in a dwindling of the movement. But, generally speaking, the creation of 640 environmental NGOs (according to the Iran's Department of Environment) within a 10-year period shows that a serious concern about environmental issues has emerged in Iran. This is not only shown through the increased number of organizations, but also through their ideological orientations and levels of activities.

The monolithic political system that dominated Iran from 1979 until 1997 planned and organized all types of organizations, and NGOs were rarely established. The reform movement emerged as a reaction to the closed nature of civil society. Subsequent reforms have resulted in staggering changes in many aspects of Iranian society, and some changes in Iranian social structure. One of the main changes within this context has been the new state–society relationship since the mid-1990s. These changes, along with fundamental world changes in social, political, and economic structure since the early 1990s, have led to the emergence of different kinds of social movements such as the environmental movement in Iran.

Iranian environmental groups are anti-systemic because their demands cannot be easily met within existing institutional arrangements. They have evolved within a semi-authoritarian (semi-democratic) context, which enables and limits their activities. They challenge the existing norms and structures, which can lead to structural transformations. Even though Iranian environmental activists are not overtly political, the movement has provoked the ire of authorities. Their main aim is to change peoples' lifestyle, and governmental policies towards environmental issues. Most activists are not radicals, although there are some scarce radical elements within the movement.

Diversity is a striking element of the environmental movement in Iran. The groups differ in their ideology, activities, goals, and size. The ideological concerns of environmentalists vary from conservationism to challenging the social, political, and economic structure of Iranian society. In most cases a combination of different ideologies is behind their activities, whereas cultural change is their central focus. To be an environmental activist means many things. For some, it means protecting endangered species and nature conservation; these activists are concerned with bringing the natural balance back into our everyday lives. Others criticize modern lifestyles and the existing social and political order. Most NGOs are based in urban areas and concentrate on urban environmental problems, but some environmental groups pay more attention to rural areas and villages, and are mostly concerned with community development. The diverse nature of the movement enables activists to penetrate different sections of society and to gain attention and support from various sectors, institutions, and groups. This diversity helps the movement to survive.

Some environmental groups pursue clear and well-defined goals, which are followed by relevant activities. Others may not have set concrete goals, but, through an active process, have developed clearer objectives. Whereas there have been some general goals pursued by most environmental groups, for example raising consciousness about environmental issues and encouraging people to be active citizens of the social and political spheres, many groups have set unique goals such as rural development or empowerment of other environmental NGOs.

Some of the groups have faced some changes in their goals and approaches through the years and have become more professional. A few groups decided to attract more members and become more public. Some improved their collaboration with authorities, whereas others have kept their distance from official organizations.

Most groups are concerned with activities such as symbolic action on special events such as the Day of Clean Air or the Mountain Day, protests and campaigns, research and publications, holding seminars and workshops, defining and participating in projects, and lobbying with officials. However, there is no single model of an environmental group as each group represents a special form of environmental action. Such diversity can be seen as a positive attribute as it makes environmental groups explore different facets of environmentalism (Dalton 1994: 248). Moreover, the diversity of the movement brings different interests and supporters together. It is not important if the person is interested in wildlife conservation, preservation of natural resources, or challenging the political establishment, there is always an organization in which to be active.

The movement incorporates a variety of groups, from small local groups with a limited number of members to nationwide groups that are active in many regions. The number of activists within each NGO varies from 10 to 5,000 members, depending on the nature of the group. In most cases there is a membership form and an annual membership fee to be formally registered with the NGO. Although membership is mostly open to anyone, some groups follow special criteria for official membership, which is mostly related to the capabilities of the members. The loose structures of the groups allow individuals be flexible in their degree of involvement. Some become very active members; however, most pay their annual membership fee and are otherwise inactive. Groups also differ regarding their period of activity—some groups last only 1 or 2 years, whereas others have been active for more than 10 years.

All NGOs are active at the national level, and some have branches in different cities. Occasionally a few groups organize an event together or work on a same project, but usually their collaboration is symbolic, for example on special events. Moreover, many groups organize environmental festivals and seminars at which huge numbers of groups gather together. In addition, most environmentalists collaborate during protests and campaigns against destructive environmental policies. As mentioned previously, environment networks are stages for communication and lobbying at which NGOs meet.

Nonetheless, the environmental movement does not have mass support, even in the big cities. To explain this, two factors should be considered: first, motivations of the participants and, second, the political structure within which the participation takes form. As participants have not been surveyed, information about their motivations is indirect— being reported by NGO representatives. However, it seems that there are two main motivations for participation in the environmental movement. The first motivation is of a political-instrumental kind. Some environmentalists were political activists before and during the revolution. In the absence of political parties and a platform for political action, they engaged in environmental action to be active in the political sphere. In other words, their motivation for participation was political. Others hold higher educational degrees in natural sciences and have professional interests in taking environmental collective action. The second motivation is of a personal-social kind. For example, in many cases, leaders of a group hold higher education degrees in human sciences and their motivation is to bring people into the public sphere where starting an environmental collective action may be considered an achievement in terms of social status and social mobility. Interests in group work and volunteer activities, being together with like-minded people, feeling useful, opportunities for attaining new roles, participating in sociopolitical actions, making some changes in their personal life, changing the society, being part of a collective action, etc., are other motivating elements for activists in joining the movement. In most cases, a combination of the two motivations is what motivates people to join a social movement. The groups that survive are those that find a balance between political/instrumental and personal/social needs (see Gross *et al.* 1983: 72).

Another important element when studying a social movement is the sociopolitical structure of the society and degree of political tolerance. Because of their history (see Chapter 2), Iranians are familiar with political protests, campaigns, and movements. Environmentalism remains an odd and unknown concept to most segments of society. Because of this unfamiliarity, the environmental organizations have not tried to attract many people. Rather, they have kept their distance from the masses and have organized their actions independently. Furthermore, large segments of the population face economic problems such as unemployment, and declining living standards, so environmentalism is not a priority for them.

Moreover, within the semi-authoritarian political system of Iran, it is clear that no social movement will have the capacity to mobilize a nationwide movement. This explains why environmental movements have remained small-scale, and concentrated on local policies and environmental issues. For example, in spite of the importance of Iran's nuclear program, there is no anti-nuclear group in the country. In order to be able to survive, environmental groups follow "depoliticized politics," and "self-imposed censorship."[4] Thus, the environmental movement continues to exist, but fails to become a wider mass movement.

Core activists of the movement in all cases appear to be from the middle class. However, in many groups, the attention of the middle class environmentalists is directed towards promoting environmental awareness, mostly among lower strata of the society. Many leaders are from the educated section of society, having been educated in Europe, the USA or Canada. However, the leadership of middle class educated people is mostly surrounded by students and housewives.

Although both sexes are represented among the leadership or founders of the NGOs, the close link between feminism and environmentalism provides a good explanation for the role of media. The number of women in the leadership of the groups, as well as the huge number of women activists is outstanding. A large number of women, and feminist principles and ideologies within many organizations, is a strong indication of the role of women within the environmental movement. As a result of the policies of post-revolutionary Iran, women started to have more and more access to schooling and education. This has led to women being involved in activities beyond their traditional roles. The increased participation of women in many spheres of social life is astonishing. A good example is the huge presence of female activists in recent uprisings since the electoral fraud of June 2009 (see Chapter 2). Despite all the restrictions imposed on women after the revolution, and regardless of the dominant traditional culture that suppressed women (before and after the revolution), the revolution and its aftermath has made it possible for women to find their way in the society.

The Islamic government gradually provided educational facilities in smaller cities and in rural and tribal areas. Electricity and telephones were provided in remote areas. Newly constructed roads connected towns and villages. Azad University (a semi-private university) opened branches in many small towns, and helped people in deprived regions gain access to knowledge and culture, despite its low quality. The numbers of pupils increased from 8 million in 1978–9 on the eve of the revolution, to 18.5 million in 1998–9 (the rate of increase: 5.5 percent per year).The number of students has risen by 1.5 million a year (a growth rate of 900 percent) (Khosrokhavar 2004). In rural areas, where girls were not allowed to attend school and university before the revolution, because wearing a scarf became compulsory and genders were segregated after the revolution, girls could attend schools and universities (Khosrokhavar 2004). As a result of these policies an educated generation emerged in which girls performed better than boys in many cases (during recent years the number of female students in universities has been higher than males). Access to higher education has taught women to think differently. Therefore, they have different demands from the previous generation. They are concerned with their individual freedom in daily life. Females are becoming more and more skeptical towards the Islamic Republic, which undermines women's rights. The new generation demands the democratization of the political sphere. They no longer demand a classless society or an Islamic society. Rather, they demand individual rights and political freedom. One environmental activist clearly explains that:

> Women have never had the chance of showing their abilities and needs. They were always considered a second sex, and were limited to their traditional roles. Today, by participating in collective action they can be part of social life. They can feel that they are doing something ... that they are changing something ...

The existing link between the women's movement and the environmental movement has been postulated as eco-feminism, a school of thought that claims that women have a closer relationship to nature than men.[5] It is claimed that the values of both movements arise from a common source (Dalton 1994: 115). Although the concept of eco-feminism might not be known among Iranian environmentalists, some interviewees gave similar reasons for the massive number of women activists and their personal environmental activities as women. One leader claims:

> I believe that women as the head of households have a direct connection to environmental problems. Raising their consciousness on the issue can enormously contribute to environmentalism.

Another leader states:

> Women's role in conservation of natural resources through the history is not deniable. Women have always had a close relationship to the nature. In Iran the traditional roles of women have always made them be the main guardians of natural resources. Moreover, women have an important role in training the next generation. Being aware of their important role can bring many positive changes to society.

Moreover, many groups pay special attention to the younger generation and at the same time have many students members. Thus, in addition to the overlap with the women's movement, the environmental movement is linked to the student movement.

Concerning the activists' relationship to the government there is a paradoxical attitude among the actors. On the one hand, the environmentalists

indicate that they do not have any serious problems with the government. However, on the other, they see the government and officials as
the main barrier to achieving their goals. This combination of hostility
and acceptance is a dominant feature of most environmental groups.
Furthermore, although the activists mostly aim to bring changes to society,
they are at the same time conscious of the need for self-restraint, and
in some cases cooperation with the government.

> We have so many problems with some officials. They cause us a lot
> of troubles. However, we need to collaborate with them in some
> occasions in order to be able to go on with our activities; in order
> to be able to bring some changes. Otherwise, we will not be able to
> work. There are some NGOs who accuse us of collaborating with
> the government. That is ignorance. They don't know that in cur-
> rent Iranian political system, it is not possible to ignore the officials
> and do whatever you want.[6]

Level of activity varies for movement activists. There is always a core
of the most active members who are in leadership positions. They
devote most of their time and energy to the group. In some cases, if the
group is well-off financially, they work as paid staff members. Registered members pay the membership fees and work with the group in
special occasions, and then there are members who are registered but
only take part in demonstrations or signing of petitions.

Although different NGOs pursue different goals and activities, most
believe that they have already achieved their goals to some degree.
Raising public awareness on the need to protect the environment, and
educating people and officials on environmental issues was are perceived to be the main successes. Environmental issues have become
more important, for example, numbers of environmental studies programs have dramatically increased at universities. Moreover, some
schools offer introductory environmental studies classes. Bringing
people into public life and making them active citizens is seen as the
second most important accomplishment of the activists. In some cases
protests and campaigns have been effective and have brought an end to
destructive projects and policies.

As many interviewees explained, being a member of a group for a
period of time has empowered the activists. Being part of a circle and a
network, has brought the activists close together, and has taught them
to make conscious decisions and to stand up for a common goal.

Today, the movement comprises a network of environmental NGOs
and weblogs. Although the movement experienced a repression following

the presidential election of 2005, it is still active and is among the few social movements that are tolerated to an extent by the regime. However, under Ahmadinezhad's presidency, environmental groups have distanced themselves from politics and have professionalized their activities. In some cases, in order to be able to survive and pursue their goals some leaders have moved towards compromises with their adversaries in politics. Some leaders have become less concerned with campaigns and protests, and more so with fundraising and protection of the organization. Therefore, Iranian environmental organizations must struggle to survive in the current political climate, in addition to pursuing their original goals.

Conclusion

This chapter has explored the diversity of the environmental groups in Iran. The common goal of environmentalists is implementing environmental protection and challenging the inefficiency of political institutions. Whereas in industrial countries, environmentalism reflects challenges of the industrial society; in developing countries, environmental concerns reflect other ambiguities. In the Iranian case, the emergence of environmentalism has revealed that society is in need of democratization. The environmentalists struggle to find legitimacy within the sphere of civil society.

Although because of the war, poverty, and extensive construction work (buildings and roads), nature and the environment faced extremely quick destruction after the revolution; the environmental organizations started in the late 1980s and grew in numbers parallel to the reform movement. This shows that the environmental movement is not a direct consequence of destructions or livelihood issues. Emergence of environmentalism in Iran represents appearance of an agenda, which is, unlike the previous movements, not directly political; although political opposition is combined with environmental goals.

Furthermore, emergence of environmentalism with its novel identity and modes of association reflects the structural changes that have occurred in the society. These changes have made the people, especially the educated middle class, become sensitive towards issues, which were untouched or rarely touched on previously.

5 The relevance of the Touraine/Melucci model in the Iranian context

Introduction

As was elaborated in the theoretical chapter, the main idea embodied in the tradition of new social movement theory, including the Touraine/Melucci model, rests on the assumption that the new social movements are "new" because they differ from the old labor movement. Moreover, the model emphasizes the fact that a "new" kind of society, that is "complex society" or "programmed society," has emerged, which generates different kinds of social movements from those of the "industrial society." That is why, unlike the old labor movement, the main focus of the new movements is identity issues rather than material demands.

To what extent can a European theory explain the situation in a non-European country? The main objective of this chapter is to provide an answer to this question by confronting the Touraine/Melucci model with the empirical findings from the case study, within the framework of Iranian social movements. This will demonstrate the extent to which the Touraine/Melucci model is relevant in the Iranian context. As the theoretical work of Touraine and Melucci is primarily based on the Western experience of modernity (post modernity) and civil society, these concepts and their implications in the Iranian context will be discussed in the following sections. Drawing from the first two parts of the chapter, the last part debates the new social movement theory. It is shown that although the Touraine/Melucci model is of great value in clarifying some aspects of Iranian social movements, it does not answer all questions when explaining the Iranian case.

Considerations for understanding the concept of modernity

In order to approach an argument on modernity, it is first necessary to spell out what modernity actually is. There are many definitions offered by a considerable number of scholars. However, Giddens' definition seems to be a suitable starting point for further discussion.

> As a first approximation, let us say the following: modernity refers to modes of social life or organization which emerged in Europe from about the seventeenth century onwards and which subsequently, became more or less worldwide in their influence.
>
> (Giddens 1990: 1)

Giddens' definition, as with many definitions of modernity, considers modernity to be a coherent socioeconomic and cultural project rooted in Europe. According to this viewpoint, modernity began in Greece and flourished in northwest Europe around the seventeenth century.

In recent years, serious questions have been raised about the Eurocentric nature of theories of modernity. If modernity is a totality or a totalizing epoch, as Eurocentric theorists of modernity believe (see, e.g. Wittrock 2000), it should be one and the same phenomenon all over the world (Kolb 1986).

A comprehensive reading of world history and its development shows that modernity did not emerge abruptly in the middle of the seventeenth century in Europe. Europe did not provide all the conditions and necessary dynamics for its development from within itself. Modernity operated across several centuries, and has followed an uneven and slow path. Many societies and their interactions have been part of this process. The early expansion of European empires, their encounters with new peoples and civilizations, and the harnessing of these to the dynamic development of Europe through conquest and colonization are important factors in the formation of the contemporary world. The process of modernity went through global conditions. However, these global, non-European dynamics and interconnections are often neglected (Hall *et al.* 1996).

Thus, it does not make sense to say that modernity started at a particular moment, nor to believe that it has followed a linear developmental pattern. The modern nation-state, which dates back to ancient Greece and the Roman Empire, for example, has a different history and time in comparison with the economic capitalist state and societies. Moreover, because different non-European societies followed (follow) different processes of historical development, it is absurd to prescribe an inevitable logic and development trajectory for all. So, considering modernity as a unity becomes an irrelevant argument (Hall *et al.* 1996).

From this perspective, Wittrock (2000) suggests that there is no such thing as European or Western modernity because they represent a mixture of elements. He emphasizes various existing institutional and cultural forms globally, and in the European context as well. Therefore, we cannot assume that a comprehensive, totalizing civilizational form will encompass all these differences and lead to homogenization of all societies. However, as modernity has now become a global condition that influences the world, in different ways, it is a common condition.

In a similar way Bernard Yack claims that:

> Modernity, the modern condition, the spirit of modern life, these are intellectual inventions inspired by our need to come to grips with the unprecedented social and cultural transformations of recent centuries. We come up with these ideas by focusing our attention on the most distinctive features of recent social experience and by consciously abstracting from the great range of ideas and institutions that do not share these features. But by treating modernity as a coherent and integrated whole, we turn these distinguishing features of social life and thought into a condition that shapes all aspects of modern experience. In this way, our own intellectual inventions, come back to haunt us as an omnipresent force in our lives.
>
> (Yack 1997: 7)

Therefore, we can say that heterotopic experiences of peoples and cultures provided different contexts of modernity. Whereas Europeans started to form their modern identity in relation to their non-Western heterotopias, the rest of the world were forced to redefine themselves in relation to Europe. The universalistic claim of introducing European modes of self-refashioning rational and modern, enabled Europeans to dismiss the heterotopic context of their self-making and consequently introduce themselves as the originators of modernity (Tavakoli-Targhi 2001).

In the mid-nineteenth century, Europe was making rapid scientific and technological advancements. Moreover, many nations all over the world were subjected to colonialism and a few major Western countries ruled the world. This is when Europe started to become a supreme model for other nations, and attempts were made to imitate Europe and its development process. However, these processes did not follow only one path.

One of the most convincing explanations to explain the trends and transformations that occurred in many societies is the concept of "multiple modernities," which was presented by Shmuel Eisenstadt (2003). Although in his understanding of the term "multiple modernities" he follows a Eurocentric view, which regards modernity as a European achievement, it rejects the view of the history and characteristics of the modern era as in the classical theories. Moreover, it goes against the sociological analysis of classical sociologists, for example Marx, Durkheim, and Weber. Unlike the assumptions of classical sociologists, which considered modernity a homogeneity that originated in Europe, the notion of "multiple modernities" declares that the reality of different societies has been different from the homogenizing Western modernity. Although a general trend towards change started to develop, the ways non-European societies were incorporating these changes differed globally (Eisenstadt 2003). This means, according to Eisenstadt (2003: 526), modernity was first generated in Europe and then spread to many places. However, this expansion of European modernity did not give rise to only one institutional pattern, but to different institutional patterns, or as Eisenstadt calls them "civilizational patterns," with different institutions or ideologies (Eisenstadt 2003: 526).

With the notion of multiple modernities, therefore, Eisenstadt suggests that in order to be able to understand the ongoing processes of the contemporary world we should deal with modernity as a "continual constitution, and reconstitution of a multiplicity of cultural programs" (Eisenstadt 2003: 536).

To show that modernity cannot be understood as unitary linear development, the multiplicity of the cultural and political programs of modernity should be taken into account. As Kaya argues, multiplicity is imbedded in modernity. He argues that although a totalizing tendency in modernity has been one dominant trend, there has always been another side emphasizing pluralism and different modes of life. Furthermore, there have always been variations in understanding the totalizing and pluralistic perceptions of modernity (see Kaya 2004a, 2004b).

For example, the rights to freedom of speech, to membership in associations, to protest and to participate in social movements are elements of the political program of modernity. These require human beings to be critical and make it impossible to be identical. Thus, the emergence of multiplicity is unavoidable (Kaya 2004b).

However, multiplicity in modernity does not mean that modernity has no uniting characteristics. Human beings' "rational mastery" and "autonomy" are two important factors of modernity. Modernity has altered the perception of human beings regarding their autonomy as it contains a strong component of reflexivity and uncertainty about basic authoritarian elements (Eisenstadt 2003: 46–7). Nevertheless, in order to argue for the concept of multiple modernities we need to show that, unlike what is believed by many theorists of modernity such as Heiddeger and Marcuse, "autonomy" and "mastery" do not have only one meaning and can be interpreted in multiple ways, depending on the subjects. This means modernity is an open concept with different interpretations. However, this openness is limited to the inclusion of mastery and autonomy of human beings, as these two concepts have different meanings for different people in different societal settings (Kaya 2004a).

Therefore, we should avoid the Eurocentric understanding of modernity as conceptualized by theorists of modernity such as Marx, Hegel, Weber, and Habermas, who tried to emphasize the uniqueness of capitalism and modernity by referring to European modernity and European social structure. Kaya (2004a: 42) argues that "modernity does not provide fixed ways of doing things, but provides the condition for interpretation." That is why the existing social theory, which is based on the West's experience with modernity, fails to provide a framework for understanding the situation in non-European (non-Western) societies.

Similar to many other societies, ideologies and institutions were brought to Iran from Europe, in the name of modernity. However, these ideologies and institutions were adapted to local conditions and, in some cases, were radically transformed. Therefore, Iran's experience of modernity was forged through a dialectical relation between the forcing powers of European modernity and the contextual realities of Iranian society. Iran never adopted the European version of modernity, although it was very much influenced by it.

Iran underwent different economic, social, and political processes to those of the European Renaissance and Enlightenment. In the final decades of the nineteenth century, new generations of social activists started to establish ideological foundations necessary for change and reform. As a result of these efforts, the foundations of modernity were shaped as a transformatory process. During this time, the political dimensions of European modernity (ideas of freedom, equality, rule of law, etc.) were introduced in order to challenge social underdevelopment and despotic monarchy (Behnam 2004).

During this time, when such concepts were being introduced to the Iranian political system, the social and cultural structures of society were different from those of eighteenth and nineteenth century Europe, which marks the time of flourishing European modernity. At the beginning of the twentieth century Iran was still an unindustrialized society under constant threat from foreign powers.

The constitutional movement was the first collective attempt to internalize the European idea of modernity in Iran. This internalization went hand in hand with implementation of modernization programs by the state at different stages of history. However, Iranian modernization did not have a single linear trajectory (Mirsepassi 2000: 10). Reza Shah, for example, fostered industrialization, cultural Westernization, established a national unity government, and centralized bureaucracy, which was accompanied by neglect of the political components of modernity (Behnam 2004).

Until the 1960s and 1970s, Iranian society achieved considerable social and economic gains. However, because of the dominant discourse of Westernization (especially during the reign of Mohammad Reza Shah), modernity started to be seen as equal to Westernization. After the revolution of 1979, the first post-revolution decade was spent on returning to the Islamic past, rejecting the West, and rejecting the influence of European modernity. It was only in the late 1980s, after the Iran–Iraq war and the death of Khomeini, that Iranians started to refer to discourses such as democracy and civil society, as components of European modernity (Behnam 2004).

In general, religion, religious institutions, and values always remained an inseparable part of Iranian society and politics (even under Reza Shah, who tried to decrease religious influences of all kinds, ulama and religious institutions remained an important pillar of society). Moreover, as the state had mistaken "modernity" with "modernization programs" imposed from above, certain changes occurred very rapidly at some historical stages, and many people remained alienated by the discourse of modernity.

Above all, democracy and the public sphere, which were some of the most important promises of European modernity, were always problematic in Iran. Although modern institutions have been introduced, and society and the economy have faced rapid changes, the political system has remained dictatorial, dependent on foreign powers, and repressive. In other words, the old tyrannical system of political rule has not changed, but continued and been embedded into the new institutions.

New institutions have emerged, but not modern mediating institutions in the European sense, such as independent newspapers, political parties, city councils, etc. Accordingly, although a series of independent newspapers, journals, and voluntary associations, which started to flourish at the time of the constitutional movement, continued and were reinforced during particular periods, the undemocratic nature of the state never allowed the public sphere to grow in its Habermasian sense.

That explains why the notion of subject, as developed in the Touraine/ Melucci model, which is embodied in the European experience of Enlightenment and considers the autonomous individual as the only source and subject of value and the center of modern society, did not emerge in Iran. The "state" and "religion" remained the most powerful and dominant institutions in Iranian society.

Considerations for understanding the concept of civil society

The concept of civil society as discussed in new social movement theory is an old concept, which has its roots in European history. However, because the history of the nation-state and civil society in Europe is entirely different from Iran, these concepts have manifested differently in Iran. Thus, application of the concepts of state and civil society (in the European sense) in the Iranian context remains problematic.

Civil society is an old concept in Western countries, although a relatively new concept in Iran. As mentioned in Chapter 3, it was during the constitutional revolution, that is about a hundred years ago, that this concept became part of the sociopolitical discourse in Iran. However, the concept only gained serious attention in the public and political discourse around a decade ago.

Iranians have never had a free and independent civil society as Europeans did (do). Unlike Europe, where much of the social praxis of associations started to take place in public spaces like coffeehouses, which were the meeting places for associations and societies (according to Habermas, these spaces support a theory of civil society as a network of associations, linking the communicative structures of the public sphere in the private "life world," which is the sphere between state and economy), in Iran the public sphere has always been restricted.

Since the constitutional revolution, there have always been associations—legal or illegal—that opposed the political system. However, a public sphere in the Habermasian sense never emerged. According to Habermas, two important aspects need to be fulfilled in order for a public sphere to be effective (Pickvance 1998): firstly, basic rights such as a free press, freedom of assembly and association, and freedom of speech and opinion have to be guaranteed by the state. Secondly, the state should control the organizations in order to make sure that these basic rights are guaranteed. Thus the public sphere, which is part of civil society in Habermas' definition, is dependent on state guarantees.

As was explained in Chapter 3, after 1997, Khatami attempted to institutionalize democracy and civil society. During Khatami's presidency the main goal of the state—although not always successful—was to guarantee citizen participation in the public sphere. Thus, it can be argued that in this period Habermas' criteria were fulfilled. However, since 2005, following the change of government, the trend was reversed. After election of Ahmadinezhad, the struggle for civil society entered a crucial phase. Established civil society organizations attempted to maintain their existence through redefining their goals and tasks. Some civil society organizations had to cease operations after the imposition of the new rules and regulations by the state. A large number have been demobilized since the 2005 presidential election. Moreover, many of the weak organizations disappeared because they were not strong enough to defend themselves against the new regulations. Likewise, some very strong civil society organizations were shut down by the government.

This shows that because civil society and its organizations are not institutionalized in Iran, when the state does not guarantee citizen participation in the public sphere, the lack of development of institutions in the public sphere can seriously hinder development of civil society. In such context, civil society can exist, but it is ineffective. Hence, Habermas' criteria cannot be met.

If we compare the period when the concept of civil society emerged and grew in Western Europe, with the current situation in Iranian society, we find some similarities and some distinct differences. In Western Europe, civil society became a relevant concept at the time when financial and commercial capitalism emerged, and the elements of a new social order were taking shape (Pickvance 1998: 203). So two parallel processes occurred simultaneously: the development of capitalism in the economic sphere and the restructuring of the political sphere. Consequently, the character of the ruling authorities was changing. Moreover, the public could challenge the state, and radical social changes occurred (Pickvance 1998: 203).

Over the past 100 years, socioeconomic and political changes in the Middle East have resulted from emergence of a civil society similar to that in Western Europe. However, as the realities of democratic development and the state–society relationship in Iran are different from those in Western societies, the civil society has developed differently.

Because the notion of civil society, as presented in new social movement theory, emerged and grew within the context of a modern European political program, it is only within this framework that we can study the European notion of civil society. This allows us to explore the ways in which people were, or are, given voice in European countries. Moreover, it provides a framework to compare Iranian civil society with its European counterpart. As mentioned above, although modernity from a sociological point of view is a Eurocentric notion, conceived to describe the social situation in Western Europe after the English Industrial and French Revolutions, the notion was later expanded to other parts of the world. Within this framework, modernity describes changes occurring in human relations in traditional communities and the creation of nation states and the new economic, political and cultural roles created for humans. A major turning point in modernity in Europe was the emergence of the public sphere, the separation of state and society, and the changing character of their relationship.

A radical transformation in European modernity resulted from new conceptions and promises of politics. At the center of the new conceptions was the breakdown of the traditional political order, opening up possibilities for the construction of a new order, and the resulting contestations for construction of the political order. These contestations were closely connected with the characteristics of European modern politics (Eisenstadt 2001).

Three main characteristics of the modern political process emerged in Europe: the combination of ideology, the premises of the political program of modernity, and the characteristics of modern political institutions. The first characteristic was the tendency to politicize the demands of various sectors of society and the conflicts between them. The second characteristic was the struggle about the definition of the realm of the political, and the third characteristic was the restructuring of center–periphery relations as the central focus of the politics (Eisenstadt 2001).

The notion of weak and strong civil society can contribute to understanding of these processes. Mouzelis (1995: 225) argues that when the process of modernization leads to an extensive spread of civil and political rights and accommodates the lower classes in a relatively autonomous manner, there is a strong civil society. In cases where such rights are not broadly spread, that is when authoritarianism prevails, there is a weak civil society. Next, he explains that a strong civil society entails the existence of rule of law effectively protecting citizens from state arbitrariness, the existence of well-organized non-state interest groups capable of checking abuses of power by those who control the means of administration and coercion, and the existence of a balanced pluralism among civil society interests so that no-one can become dominant (Mouzelis 1995: 225–26).

Although studying the notion of civil society within the framework of European modernity contributes to an understanding of the concept as it emerged in Europe, in order to gain a comprehensive understanding of civil society in Iran we must take into account characteristics of Iranian society, especially those related to the state–society relationship.

Many studies analyzing the internal dynamics of non-Western societies fail to pay adequate attention to the differences in culture and power relations, and the challenges to the hegemonic relations and discourses (Eisenstadt 2003: 406). However, with respect to analyzing the relationship between culture and power, analyzing the public sphere becomes important because public spheres and social movements are among the most important institutional arenas in which rulers, elites, and various social groups negotiate the definition of common good and legitimation, accountability of authorities, and possible challenges to the existing hegemonies (Eisenstadt 2003: 409).

For example, in Muslim societies, although rulers have always been crucial for maintenance of public order and of the community, they have never been seen as regulators of public life. It was the ulama who were the guardians of public life and Islamic community, upholders of normative dimensions of the umma (Islamic community or nation), and keepers and interpreters of the sharia. The central role played by ulama in Muslim societies distinguishes the Muslim regimes and societies from other societies (Eisenstadt 2003: 414). Ulama created networks within which various ethnic groups were gathered. Moreover, they were an important element in forming the characteristics of public spheres in Islamic societies by providing spheres of life that were not controllable by the rulers. These public spheres were areas in which different sectors of society could voice their demands in the name of the basic premises (Eisenstadt 2003: 415).

Therefore, it was the continual interaction between the rulers, ulama and different sections of society that constituted an autonomous public sphere in Islamic societies (Eisenstadt 2003: 415). However, as Eisenstadt argues, the autonomy of the ulama, the hegemony of sharia, and the vitality of public spheres in Muslim society do not imply autonomous access to the ruling classes. He claims that in Muslim societies a "decoupling" occurred between the structure of the public sphere and the decision making of the rulers. On one hand, limited autonomy was given to large segments of society to make policy, and, on the other, the upholding of the moral order of the community was done by ulama, and the rulers played a secondary role (Eisenstadt 2003: 417).

However, despite the potential autonomy of members of ulama, fully institutionalized and effective control of the rulers did not develop in these societies. That is why the only way to enforce any radical political demand remained through rebellious actions (Eisenstadt 2003: 421).

In the case of Iran, these processes and trends have been uneven. As Mirsepassi (2000: 74) explained, the economic and social relations of society have changed radically since the beginning of the twentieth century, through modernization programs. Conversely, peoples' participation was not affected by these changes. Thus, people confronted by modernization programs were alienated from their processes. The modernization programs did not encompass change in political power structures. On the contrary, through the modernization process, a more structured and powerful autocratic state power was built. Autonomous institutions and organizations were destroyed, and all power was concentrated in the hands of the state. So, some aspects of European modernity, such as centralization of state power, modernization of the national military and police, implementation of particular means of surveillance and control, civil society organizations such as political parties, trade unions, and citizen's organizations, remained strictly under the control of state power. That is why popular and viable modern political institutions were never created in Iran. Thus, the relationship between the state and society remained unchanged (Mirsepassi 2000: 189–90).

Since the constitutional revolution, the emergence of new structures and institutions has produced imbalances in the political realm. The rapid modernization of the Pahlavi regime, for example, was not only incapable of overcoming the problems of political dysfunctions but it added to the problems, and lower layers of society remained disconnected from the process of decision making. After the revolution, because of undemocratic practices and the Iran–Iraq war, the problem remained unsolved. It was only within the process of the reform movement that empowerment of civil society and independent organizations was introduced as a solution to the blocked and disabled political system. Unlike during the revolutionary era, the goal was not to encourage the masses to participate in street protests. However, emphasis has been directed towards encouraging people to organize in associations, NGOs, councils, etc., and to find a way to actively participate in sociopolitical affairs. As has been argued, today Iran is confronted with ideas similar to those which took place in Europe during the Reformation, and Enlightenment periods (Hashemi 2004).

However, civil society has always been weak and the state has always played a very strong role in Iran. The outlook that existed in Iranian politics until recently was that society is either against or for the state. The public image of the state is that it has an unchangeable nature, and it follows an autonomous discourse. The state is either capable of doing everything for the people or is the enemy of the people. Therefore, intermediary institutions, which balance the function of the state, never seemed meaningful. Moreover, due to the tradition of authoritarianism, people see every kind of civil activity as power-oriented. Therefore, connection between the state and civil society has remained problematic.

Furthermore, the emergence and development of civil society in Europe took place over a few centuries. Industrialization and the emergence of the bourgeoisie as a social class were two important developments in Europe during this time. However, civil society as a concept is foreign to the Iranian public discourse; it does not have deep roots in Iranian society, culture, and politics. That is why Iranian society was not capable of digesting these ideas, which were in disharmony with the culture, traditions, and structures of society.

At the dawn of the twentieth century and the constitutional revolution, when the concepts of civil society and the public sphere were gradually introduced, Iranian society was still an entirely different society from Western countries. Iran was neither industrialized, nor did a bourgeois class exist. Moreover, most of the population was living in rural areas and was illiterate, and the power of the king had been widespread for many centuries, ruling many aspects of society.

Furthermore, the influence of foreign powers in Iran directed the attention of many progressive groups towards nationalism, and prevented them from focusing on the ideas of individual rights and civil society.

Moreover, as Iran is a Muslim society, the question might arise of whether it is possible to have a civil society in an Islamic society. Although some scholars have introduced Islam as a rival to civil society (Gellner 1994) because of its resistance to secularization (this is a false characterization; Turkey is a secular society, for example), the diversity of Islam and its practices offer a very different image of orthodoxy.

Although the Iranian state is considered the preserve of Islamic fundamentalists, it offers a totally different image of what is known as fundamentalism in its orthodox sense. Even though the Iranian mullahs gained power after the revolution and started to Islamize the country, for the first time in Iran's history a republic was established, with popular elections, a constituent assembly, a parliament, a president, a council of ministers, and a constitution that was a copy of the 1958 French Constitution. This is in contrast to orthodox Islam or Islamic fundamentalism (i.e. Wahabism), but similar to modern Europe in its institutional, governmental and political arrangements (Al-Azma 1997).

Although the dogmatism of the Iranian rulers in the name of Islam cannot be denied, it must be recognized that, in addition to Islamic practices, many current sociopolitical discourses are shaped by the historical experiences of Iran through the centuries and the impact of its interaction with the outside world. Redistribution of wealth, economic dependency, the fight against imperialism, development, and modernization have been part of the public discourse since the revolution.

However, unlike Europe, which experienced an era of secularization and separation of religion and state, religion and religious institutions have always played an important role in Iran. To put it differently, religion has always been one of the mediums of political expression and mobilization in Iran.

It was during the rule of the Qajar dynasty (1796–1925) that mullahs became powerful in Iranian politics. This is related to the weakness of the Qajar state, the penetration of foreign capital, and the political domination of Iran by European powers. Under such circumstances, mullahs gained the opportunity to establish themselves as defenders of nationalism and independence. At the same time, because of the Western cultural impact and the consequent trend towards secularization of the society, the mullahs' position was undermined. Some politicians attempted to reduce the influence of mullahs. However, the constant intervention of Europeans in the political and economic activities of Iran, combined with the anti-Western position of mullahs, increased their power. Moreover, the expansion of European capital and goods resulted in the decline of Iranian manufactures that threatened bazaaris. This resulted in an alliance between these two groups, which survived into the contemporary era (Amjad 1989: 37). During the Pahlavi regime, the political repression of the centralist state prevented the emergence of all forms of political and social opposition, except for religious-based opposition. That is why the clerical establishment became a necessary political and social source of inspiration for the masses before the revolution (Moshiri 1985).

There are four main conclusions drawn from comparing the civil society discourse in Iran and Europe. First, civil society should be studied in its contextual setting. It should concern different aspects of culture, society, and politics, and the interactions between them. Thus, ahistorical readings of the concept of the civil society should be rejected. It is important to realize that the countries' unique experiences provide a basis for the realities of democratic development and civil society.

Second, despite its conceptualization by Western theorists, civil society has been the dominant discourse in Iranian society for more than a decade. It has led to the rise of many civil society organizations, and new narratives and discourses (see Chapter 3).

Third, the nature of civil society in Iran has been dynamic since the beginning of the twentieth century. However, the civil society in Iran is still weak. The evolution of civil society is confronted with several restrictions as it is still not completely independent of the state. Therefore, the state challenges the nature of civil society, leading to new kinds of struggles. This is mostly because there is still no guarantee of individual and group rights to construct a legally protected public sphere. Nonetheless, Iranian civil society, although different from its European counterparts, does not have the corporatist or state-led characteristics of civil society in some countries. In order to understand the nature of civil society in Iran, we should not ignore its semi-democratic (semi-authoritarian) context. This context has led to a specific nature of state and civil society, in which social action is not a directly hostile towards the state but it is an interaction and negotiation with the state. This is totally different from an authoritarian context. The current environmental movements in Iran can only be understood in the context of a transitory civil society in a semi-democratic (semi-authoritarian) context.

The final conclusion is that a strong civil society can only develop in a democratic regime. In this regard, I agree with Habermas and his emphasis on the role of the state in guaranteeing the basic rights of organizations in public sphere. Iran is still far from a democratic progressive society, and, therefore, a strong civil society. For many years the Iranian political system has been patrimonial. This means that the power had been in the hands of one man (or a small group of men) without any possibility of controlling and limiting him/them by law. Moreover, since the constitutional revolution, many social activists have tried to limit the power of the state and to control it within the boundaries of the constitution. In other words, they have tried to implement the liberal democracy of Western societies. But in practice this kind of democracy was never implemented. The novelty of the reform movement of Iran, therefore, lies in the fact that it views democracy as a double-sided process. On one hand, it is concerned with the reform of state power, and on the other, with the restructuring of civil society (Held 2006). So the transformation of both state and civil society becomes crucial in the process of democratization. The establishment of a civil and democratic society is a process that might take hundreds of years, as in Europe. The Iranian society and politics need to internalize democracy and, to do this, an open space is necessary for dialogue, critical ideas and respect for the rights of individuals, or, in other words, a democratic culture. And, until that day, paradoxes, illusions, and contradictions of state and society are unavoidable (Seddighi 2001).

Considerations for understanding (new) social movements

In theories of new social movements, particularly the Touraine/Melucci model, old movements and new movements have been understood as two distinct kinds of social movements. The old movements are associated with the ideals and norms of industrialism, and focus on economic issues and the state. As Eisenstadt (2003: 853) argues, the characteristics of the labor movement in Europe were closely linked to certain premises of European modernity, namely, the combination of protest and institution formation, the quest to broaden the scope of participation and the combination of political struggle and intellectual heterodoxy.

Advancements in Western industrialized societies, and the emergence of post-industrial society, which has generated "different" kinds of movements from those of the industrial society, were the starting points for further assumptions of new social movement theorists. The new social movements were perceived as successors of the old movements. These movements are different from the old left in the sense that they are not led by the social democratic or communist parties or the trade unions (see e.g. Cleveland 2003). The identity, forms of organization, and goals of the new social movements are results of the post-material age. The assumption is that the new movements of post-industrial society replace the old movements of industrial society.

If we believe this assumption, that social movements (old and new) emerge only in industrial or post-industrial society, this means that other parts of the world that did not experience industrialization and post industrialization cannot have social movements! Moreover, as Scott (1990: 80) has argued, in the contemporary world there are hardly any countries that are post industrialized, programmed, and information-based, as Melucci believes. Instead, there is a degree of post industrialism, or programming, in each society. So being programmed or not is a relative concept and cannot be defined in absolute terms (Scott 1990: 80).

Additionally, the Touraine/Melucci model requires many conditions for new social movements to arise. The conditions under which the notion of subject has emerged, the assumptions of state–society relationships and democracy, are all rooted and defined through the framework of European modernity. Hence, at first glance, it is problematic to consider the European Enlightenment as the prerequisite for understanding the essence of (new) social movements.

The anti-capitalist movements of industrial societies were consequences of rapid capitalism and industrialization. That is why these movements are emblematic of the old movements in industrial societies. However, Iran has never been an industrial society in the European sense. The growth of capitalism has followed a much slower pace than that of an industrialized country, and, therefore, the working class have very different characteristics from the working class in Europe. Although Iran experienced a communist movement and a communist party, communism never became popular in Iran. The communist movement started during the constitutional movement and continued after the victory of the constitutional revolution. A communist party was established after the abdication of Reza Shah in 1941 (the Tudeh Party, which was one of the most influential communist parties of the Middle East). Even though the communists played important roles in mobilizing people in two grand social movements of the century, the national oil movement and the revolutionary movement of 1979, unlike their Western counterparts, they never developed into a central movement.

Moreover, because of its history, Iran's social movements have been anti-imperialist and anti-authoritarian instead of anti-capitalist. Therefore, in contrast with their European counterparts, the middle class, rather than the working class, was the protagonist of old social movements in Iran. Therefore, the newness of current Iranian social movements, for example the environmental movement, cannot be explained by referring to the characteristics of industrialized societies and the workers' movement.

As the new social movement theory's primary assumption links emergence of the new social movements to the characteristics of post-industrial society, Melucci suggests that the environmental issues in the West proclaim at least four characteristics of a transformed society. He states that:

> Ecological issues are a systemic problem, which reveals behind its surface the phenomenon of a planetary interdependence that creates

new frontiers of human consciousness, and action. Furthermore, it highlights the cultural dimensions of human action. The industrial society was centered on the inevitability of economic laws and technical power. The ecological issue shows that our salvation lies no anymore in the system of means founded on purposive rationality but in the system of ends i.e. cultural models, that orient our behavior. It is a signal that the individual has come to a point to produce its sphere of action. Thirdly, environmental problems affect individuals qua individuals and not as member of a group, class or a state. It is evident that the future of the ecosystem will affect the life of each of us. Thus, change can no longer be dissociated from individual responsibility. Direct and personal effort has become a resource for intervention in the system. Finally, the ecological question signals that conflict is a physiological dimension of complex systems. While in the industrial culture conflict considered to emerge as the necessary outcome of exploitation or a social pathology, in a complex society the differentiation of interests and of cultures and uncertainty as the constant condition of human action, give rise to an ineradicable quota of conflict in social life.

(Melucci 1989: 58–9)

Although the challenge faced by Iranian environmentalists is to the dominant paradigm, it reveals that society has gone through structural transformations, and the new social movement theory, with its European assumptions focusing on the importance of post-materialistic values, does not provide a comprehensive explanation for the emergence and evolution of the environmental movement in Iran.

Instead, the emergence of environmentalism in Iran is a combination of different factors such as extreme environmental destructions, changes in Iran's social structure and politics, globalization and the increasing role of the media in the everyday lives, rise of environmentalism as a global issue, and, above all, the emergence of the reform movement and a new public discourse.

Moreover, post-materialist and anti-consumptionist values, which are the most important sets of attitudes embodied in the European new social movements, are only one aspect of the Iranian environmental movement due to the lower level of industrialization and capitalist development compared with Europe. Therefore, unlike new social movements of Europe, which in Habermas' words were organized against the "colonization of the life world," the new social movements of Iran, including the environmental movement, challenge the dominant culture of the Islamic Republic and its influence on their everyday lives. The movements struggle for new identities and cultural codes (Yaghmaian 2002).

One of the main goals of the Islamic Republic from the beginning was cultural transformation of society by the creation of hegemonic Islamic social and cultural norms. Opposition to "modern" and "Western" sociocultural values was the main focus of the Islamization process. Nonetheless, two decades after the victory of the revolution, social movements arose that were against the state's cultural project of homogeneity and different kinds of collective action for rights (Yaghmaian 2002). Environmentalists focus on the experiences of everyday life. They are people who embrace alternative ways of life and behaviors and seek new kinds of rights.

The environmental movement in Iran started as part of the pro-democracy (reform) movement, with goals of broadening the scope of citizenship rights and civil society, which are goals of the old movements according to Touraine/Melucci. The reform movement of Iran is not a specific-issue movement like many contemporary European movements. It is a general movement, opposing the dominant political structure of the society. Its critique of the dominant discourse has been holistic. It focuses on new principles and programs, and its ultimate aim is to introduce a new order in society. In other words, the reform movement is a social movement that seeks to establish autonomy from civil life. It also emphasizes the affirmation of rights of the social actor and transformation of the existing situation. At the same time, the reform movement gave rise to some specific-issue movements, such as the environment and women's movements. The environmental movement, as an example of a specific-issue movement, in contrast, focuses on the formation of new identities, norms, and life styles, which are promises of the new social movements, according to new social movement theory.

Moreover, as was demonstrated before, the environmental movement functions under different circumstances and faces different limitations from those of their European counterparts. The semi-authoritarian political system and its internal conflicts, the undefined nature of civil society organizations and the cultural, demographic, and economic problems, have limited the activities of the environmentalists in Iran (see Chapter 4). Furthermore, because of the nature of Iranian society and state, which was discussed before, the environmental movement is not entirely independent from the state. The movement mostly functions through NGOs, which are registered with governmental bodies.

However, although partly directed towards the state and its challenges, the identity, their organization, and goals of the environmentalists are novel in the history of Iranian social movements. The newness of Iranian environmentalism can be explained if we compare this with the previous social movements of Iran. The Iranian environmental movement emerged from the reform movement, which was a distinct social movement, and the last grand social movement in modern Iran (see Chapter 3).

As explained by Cleveland (2003), the Iranian environmental movement is led by intellectuals in the Gramscian sense of the word, that is people who try to educate the masses about how to successfully fight oppression. These environmentalist intellectuals belong to the middle class, and they are mostly from the university or are former university students. That is why the environmental movement overlaps with student and women's movements. Women and youth play an important role in the leadership and body of the movement.

Considering the social movements of twentieth century in Iran, we can identify two main sources of social conflict that led to emergence of social movements: state/citizens and nation/imperialism cleavages. The reform movement emerged around the state/citizen conflict. But a new set of movements arose from this, which are mostly concerned with cultural issues. Environmentalism emerged from a movement centered on traditional grievances, but it raised new grievances itself.

Finally, environmentalists do not express themselves through direct political action, but they raise challenges to the dominant social practices. Their main aim is to increase their influence on public opinion and the authorities. Changing life style and searching for innovative ways of civil participation are examples of the new challenges they raise. However, environmentalism criticizes the prevailing political order in a different way from previous movements. Environmentalists do not seek to take over control of the state and economy, but similar to the Western new social movements, they challenge the boundaries of conventional politics (see Cleveland 2003).

Therefore, as Melucci (1996a) believes, the environmental movements have pre-political and meta-political qualities. In the Iranian political system, similar to Melucci's analysis of Italian society, the most important factor is the presence of the state in all aspects of Iranians' daily lives, which has led to the "hyper-politicization" of social action. However, autonomous civil initiatives are relatively limited and the political system is viewed as illegitimate. The "hyper-politicization" and "under-representation" of social action, therefore, have resulted in suffocation of the new demands of society. During

Khatami's government, although an attempt was made to create space for new demands and needs, the new movements started to seek their new social demands within the established political equilibrium because they were not allowed to go beyond it, with the resulting emergence of non-political forms of social action. This explains the pre-political aspect of the movements. At the same time, the movements demonstrate the existence of some basic dilemmas of the system, which cannot be solved through political channels. In this regard they are seen as meta-political.

However, as explained above, Iranian social movements are not located outside the sphere of politics. The nature of civil society in Iran is still fragile and not completely defined. Therefore, the separation of state and society, and the activities that are located in the sphere of civil society, are different from Europe. That is why, unlike the assumption of the new social movement theory that the new movements function separately from the state, the new Iranian movements were born out of the reform movement, which is a political movement initially inspired from within the government. The concerns of many of the new movements are still limiting the state power and its performance on many occasions. Moreover, most social movement activists are also clearly conscious of their political role. So separation of politics and civil society becomes irrelevant in the Iranian case. Therefore, considering democracy as a prerequisite for the emergence of new social movements becomes inappropriate.

In spite of these shortcomings, the Touraine/Melucci model is capable of explaining some aspects of the Iranian environmental movement. First, the increased importance of cultural dimensions of human action and the production of cultural codes, particularly the emergence of environmental concerns in Iran, reveal that a change in people's mindset has occurred. This change has planetary dimensions. There are some problems, such as environmental problems, which affect each of us as individuals directly. Moreover, it shows that there are important issues at stake in society, which are not able to be solved through already established political channels.

Second, concerning the loose structure and the composition of the movement participants (they are from the middle class and the educated strata of the society), the new social movement theory is accurate in the Iranian context.

Third, the increasing role of the media in influencing the new social movements is an important aspect of new social movement theory. Weight has been given to the role of the mass media and information technology in shaping public opinion. As was shown throughout

Chapter 4, the media played an important role in increasing the knowledge of people towards environmental issues, and in mobilizing them. However, censorship and lack of democracy has forced the media to function differently from that in Western societies.

Towards a revised model?

As was described previously, the theoretical work of Touraine/Melucci, which is based on the European experience, is incapable of providing a full analysis of Iranian social movements. However, in some ways it accurately describes the Iranian context. There are two aspects in which the Touraine/Melucci model has not been of use to our investigation.

1. Implication of the concept of modernity in its European sense, based on the writings of classical sociologists such as Marx and Weber, is not compatible with non-Western cultures and histories. It provides a one-sided idea to explain the reality of our complex world, and, in particular, Iranian society. Instead of modernity we should be talking about modernities. Consequently, the emphasis on social structures of industrial and post-industrial societies, and the role of labor movements and their replacement by new social movements, is not relevant in the case of Iran.
2. Locating the new movements outside the sphere of politics, but in civil society and the public sphere, is another shortcoming of the model. Although concepts of civil society and the public sphere are useful in analyzing the social movements, this does not mean that these concepts and processes are always identical. Powerful, independent public spaces, which already exist, would provide new movements with the possibilities of articulating and publicizing their needs. However, absolute existence of such independent public spheres, particularly in semi-authoritarian structures, remains problematic.

Nevertheless, there are four respects in which the Touraine/Melucci model has been useful in this study:

1. The Touraine/Melucci model tries to identify the "newness" of the new social movements by referring to structural changes in society. This level of analysis provides grounds for investigating the new Iranian movements as well. However, the criteria of the shift from the industrial to post-industrial society does not provide a starting point for the analysis of Iranian (new) social movements.

2. The second point refers to the growing importance of cultural aspects of social action, which has become the dominant aspect of new social movements. Producing cultural codes, and changing the meaning of social life, has become part of the reality of new social movements.

3. Globalization, and resulting interconnections all over the world, has brought about some general values and levels of organization in most parts of the world. For this reason post-materialist and anti-consumptionist attitudes embedded in the European new social movements are of significance in the Iranian new movements. Therefore, as Melucci (1989) claims, in our "globally interdependent" societies, "global social problems" have emerged. Moreover, the loose structure of the movements and the composition of their participants are more or less identical to the European new social movements.

4. The new movements' relation to the media, and the role of the internet and the mass media in influencing the movements and public opinion have been proven relevant too. The effects of globalization have paved the way for significant progress in means of communication and social networking. The increased capability of collecting, processing, and transforming information in recent years has influenced individuals and social actions to a large extent.

In order to be able to make use of the Touraine/Melucci model in non-European contexts, we should try to combine two different levels of analysis, that is structural and conceptual. Society and social movements should be seen in terms of structures and structural transformations. However, our understanding of social structures should either be based on a few major concepts or ideas, which are general and global, or it should limit itself to a specific region or historical context. The latter should then consider the relativity of various concepts in different social settings. This can provide a starting point for further understandings and hypotheses about social movements.

The most practical way, however, is to combine the model with the configurational approach (Rehbein 2007). As Rehbein (2007: 26) argues:

> The configurational approach is situated at an intermediate level of social reality, theory and methodology. Every new insight and concept can alter the whole picture. The configuration is multi-dimensional and open, dialectical and relational. No element can be defined ultimately and independently, but in relation to the

other elements of the configuration. Therefore, the main virtue of the configurational approach is the combination of systemic thinking and openness.

Taking into account the above considerations, it is possible to develop the theoretical model of Touraine/Melucci with regards to their focus on the two concepts of modernity and civil society. However, we need to understand these two concepts differently. In other words, we need to go beyond Touraine/Melucci's interpretation of these two concepts. Therefore, the following interconnected considerations should be taken into account.

Social structures should not be seen as homologous entities. Beneath the social structures lie the historical past, different trends of modernity, and various types of globalization (this is different from the Eurocentric and container model of society). There is not just one modernity, but multiple modernities, so a broad understanding of modernity is much more useful in interpreting the reality of different societies. In this way we can relate the concept of modernity to concepts such as power relations, social structure, culture, and economics. Furthermore, various types of globalization and their implications in different contexts should be taken into account. What we need to do in this regard is to permanently deal with this question: how does globalization influence social structures and cultures? Therefore, the concept of civil society and its implications should be understood in relation to the three settings of historical past, modernity, and globalization. Any unconditional interpretation of this concept and its relationship to social movements should be avoided.

Conclusion

The Touraine/Melucci model focuses on the fact that some European concepts and structures have universal validity and can be used as a basis for further analysis of social phenomena, for example social movements all over the world. In this regard, their main attention is on the relationship between social structures, changes in social structures and social movements. However, social structure is not a fixed entity but a fluid concept and cannot be understood unconditionally. Different parts of the world have experienced modernization and development differently, and these experiences are not similar to the path explained by the Touraine/Melucci model. Consequently, societies have experienced different social, cultural, and political structures and transformations.

Above all, globalization processes are undermining the importance of national state, and this has led to the emergence of some global structures and the collapse of old concepts. For example, as Ulrich Beck (2005: 24) claims, the image of "modern", organized individual societies, which was a totally necessary concept in the work of classical sociologists, has been shaken by concepts such as globality and globalization. That is why a convincing theory of social movements should go beyond the container model and European history. Rather, it should focus on the current global and multi-dimensional world. Furthermore, the concepts chosen to explain and analyze social structures should be seen in dynamic ways and through mechanisms that are global and general, rather than static concepts or specific mechanisms.

6 Conclusions

In this study, I intended to address three interconnected issues: firstly, to explore the development of modern Iranian social movements to see if there is any continuity or similarity in their essence and nature; secondly, to present an in-depth study of the Iranian environmental movement as an example of a new social movement; and, finally, to examine the relevance of the Touraine/Melucci model in the Iranian context. The objective of this chapter is to see whether or not I have achieved these aims. The final sentences of this study are dedicated to some recommendations for understanding Iranian society.

In relation to the first aim, I provided an overview of four grand social movements of modern Iran. Most of the previous studies of Iranian social movements have focused on only one or two of these movements, without any attempt to compare them in order to find similarities or differences. The systematic analysis provided here has offered a wider context for understanding the nature of Iranian social movements. Moreover, it has paved the way for better understanding of the ongoing reform movement.

I demonstrated that an environmental movement has emerged in Iran. Moreover, I have placed this movement within the historical context of preceding twentieth-century movements. Furthermore, I stated that the environmental movement is a "new" kind of social movement in the history of modern Iranian social movements. I provided an empirical study of the Iranian environmental movement referring to the core of the movement (Tehran), and an example of the periphery (Rasht). Emergence, modes of action, identity, goals, and the limitations of the movement were discussed in detail. This is an original contribution because previous studies of Iranian social movements have not presented such an empirical study on environmentalism. Moreover, the case of environmental movements can be seen as a base for gaining a broad understanding of other forms of social movements in contemporary Iran.

Third, considerable attention has been given to the relevance of the Touraine/Melucci model in the Iranian context. Two major arguments have been developed.

Firstly, the Touraine/Melucci model is set within the European context, focusing on the European concepts of modernity and civil society. This prevents it from providing a comprehensive understanding of non-European societies, such as Iran, with different social and historical backgrounds. Although the focus on structural changes and social transformations of the society can be relevant in explaining the emergence of the Iranian environmental movement, it does not mean that the changes are identical to those occurring Europe. Therefore, the model does not explain the whole reality, and must be revised in some respects. A configurational approach has been suggested as a solution to overcome some of these limitations.

Secondly, despite its European nature and origin, and regardless of its shortcomings, this model is useful in explaining some aspects of Iranian society and its social movements. Its emphasis on the importance of societal transformations for the emergence of new kinds of movements is of the great relevance to the Iranian context. Moreover, this contributes to the emergence of a "planetary system," as described by Melucci, and nothing and nobody is external to this. This explains why some aspects of contemporary Iranian social movements can be partially explained by European approaches. Thus, in the era of globalization, fully isolated entities do not exist.

The final conclusions of this study include two recommendations for studying Iranian society.

The first conclusion is that there exist different experiences of modernity, civil society, social movements, and, in a broader scope, social change. In order to be able to understand the reality of Iranian society, we need to view the situation as different from that in Europe. Although there are some universal concepts, such as civil society or social movements, which help us to discover and analyze the reality of different societies, this does not mean that these concepts are similar in all societies of the world. Local circumstances shape and influence social structures, and, consequently, social actions should be taken into account.

Iran is facing a new era, which has brought with it new demands, and allowed for new kinds of social action. The emergence of new kinds of movements is one of the first indications that Iran's cultural, social, and political boundaries are changing. That is why in-depth studies of contemporary social action (social movements) have become prerequisites for analyzing the new processes of social and political transformation in contemporary Iran. Although there are quite a few theoretical studies on social movements, these studies are mostly by European scholars, or based on European theoretical perspectives. More context-related social research, which contributes to broadening the already existing social theories, is a prerequisite for understanding the reality of non-Western countries.

However, Iranian scholars have not paid enough attention to this issue. They have never attempted to develop a theoretical and conceptual framework to study Iranian social movements. In order to gain a full understanding of contemporary social movements and the current societal changes in Iran, it is crucial to research Iranian society systematically.

This is, however, just the beginning. The relationship between civil society and social movements, and their particular influence on democracy and social transformations should receive more attention in sociological research. Moreover, comparative studies of the new social movements, across space or time (or a combination of both), are important.

Above all, Iran and Iranian social movements cannot be understood without being situated in globalization. For this reason it is necessary to study Iranian social movements within the framework of transnational social movements. However, in order to be able to do all these, we require an advanced and convincing theoretical framework. I hope that this work contributes an introductory step towards a more comprehensive future study: "A Sociology of Social Movements in Iran."

Notes

1 Theoretical framework

1 Contemporary debates on globalization have remained bounded to the Eurocentric social theory, which is why interpretation of the concept (especially in relation to the global South) has remained problematic. Hence, as some scholars have suggested, it is better to talk about globalizations (in a plural form) or about different types of globalization. See, for example, Rehbein 2007.

2 Grand social movements of Iran in the twentieth century

1 By modern social movements I refer to the social movements of the Iranian modern era. This era started at the beginning of the twentieth century with establishment of a parliamentary state.
2 Due to the absence of one generally accepted term in English to refer to the four grand social movements that have been discussed here, I have decided not to capitalize them.
3 With the hostage crisis of 1979–81, the Iranian government's "anti-USA" officially started. The crisis began in November 1979, when a group of Islamists took over the US embassy in Tehran and 52 American diplomats were held hostage for 444 days. The hostages were released on 20 January 1981.
4 It should be mentioned that the protests and civilian activities started in the aftermath of the 2009 election are referred to as "the Green Movement." Although the mobilizations were a continuation and result of the reform movement, in the sociopolitical discourse of society they have been given a new name.

4 From a movement for civil society towards a movement for the environment

1 It should be mentioned that unlike the NGOs in a lot of developing countries, Iranian NGOs are not allowed to accept foreign aid or, most of the time, to collaborate with foreign agencies outside the country. It might be that after starting action with a foreign agency or receiving aid, the government prevents them from the continuation of their work. The NGO can be accused of spying for the country that has provided the financial aid! Therefore, in

Iran, the branches of UNDP and GEF are the most accepted international organizations with which to work.

2 An official organization established under Khatami's presidency to improve the standards of living of youth all over the country. For a period of time, the National Youth Organization encouraged the young generation to establish NGOs in different fields.

3 A cultural center established during Khatami's presidency, with the main activity of holding seminars, conferences, lectures, workshops, etc. Its establishment was related to putting into practice the idea of "dialogue among civilizations," introduced by Khatami as a response to Samuel Huntington's theory of Clash of Civilizations.

4 Similar characteristics have been observed in Chinese environmental organizations by Peter Ho and Richard Louis Edmonds (see Ho and Edmonds 2007).

5 There are two main trends in eco-feminist thoughts. First, that women and nature both create and sustain life. Second, that women and nature are both exploited within the industrial male-dominated society (see Skogen 1999).

6 Some of the interviews quoted in this chapter have been quoted in an article published by the author previously (see Fadaee 2011a).

References

Abrahamian, E. (1982) *Iran between two revolutions*, Princeton, N.J: Princeton University Press.

——(2008) *A history of modern Iran*, Cambridge: Cambridge University Press.

Alavitabar, A. (2001) 'Islam und Demokratie im Protest der Studenten', in S. Seddighi and B. Nirumand (eds) *Iran nach den Wahlen: Eine Konferenz und ihre Folgen.* Münster: Westfaelisches Dampfboot.

Al-Azma, S.J. (1997) 'Is Islam Secularizable?' in E. Özdalga and S. Persson (eds) *Civil Society, Democracy and the Muslim World.* Papers read at a conference held at the Swedish research institute in Istanbul 28–30 October 1996, Richmond: Curzon.

Alexander, J.C. (2006) *The Civil Sphere*, New York/Oxford: Oxford University Press.

Amjad, M. (1989) *Iran: from royal dictatorship to theocracy*, New York: Greenwood Press.

Ansari, A. (2003) *Modern Iran since 1921*, London [u.a]: Longman.

Arjomand, S.A. (1988) *The Turban for the Crown: The Islamic Revolution in Iran*, New York: Oxford University Press.

Ashraf, A. and Banuazizi, A. (1985) 'The State, Classes and Modes of Mobilization in the Iranian Revolution', *State, Culture and Society* 1:3–40.

Avritzer, L. and Lyyra, T. (1997) 'New Cultures, Social Movements and the Role of Knowledge: An Interview with Alberto Melucci', *Thesis Eleven* 48: 91–109.

Barnameye azme meli baraye hefazat az mohite zist (1999). Tehran: Entesharate sazmane hefazate mohite zist.

Bayat, M. (1991) *Iran's first revolution: Shi'ism and the constitutional revolution of 1905–1909*, New York: Oxford University Press.

Beck, U. (2005) *what is Globalization?*, Cambridge [u.a.]: Polity Press.

Behnam, J. (2004) 'Iranian Society, Modernity and Globalization', in R. Jahanbegloo (ed.) *Iran: Between Tradition and Modernity*, Lanham, MD: Lextington books.

Behrooz, M. (2000) *Rebels with a Cause: The Failure of the Left in Iran*, London [u.a]: Tauris.

Blumer, H. (1951) 'Collective Behavior', in A. M. Lee *et al.* (eds) *New Outlines of the Principles of Sociology*, New York: Barnes & Noble.

Boggs, C. (1987) *Social movements and political power: emerging forms of radicalism in the West*, Philadelphia: Temple University Press.

Brumberg, D.M. (2001) *Reinventing Khomeini: the struggle for reform in Iran*, Chicago/London: University of Chicago Press.

Castells, M. (1998) *End of Millennium*, Cambridge, MA/Oxford, UK: Blackwell Publishers.

——(2004) *The Power of Identity*, Oxford: Blackwell.

Clawson, P. and Rubin, M. (2006) *Eternal Iran: Continuity and Chaos*, Basingstoke: Palgrave Macmillan.

Cleveland, J.W. (2003) 'Does the New Middle Class Lead Today's Social Movements?', *Critical Sociology* (29): 163–90.

Cohen, J. (1985) Strategy of Identity: new theoretical paradigms and contemporary social movements, *Social Research* 52: 663–719.

——(1996) 'Mobilization, Politics and Civil Society: Alain Touraine and Social Movements', in J. Clarck and M. Diani (eds), *Alain Touraine*, London and Washington, DC: Falmer Press.

Cronin, S. (ed.) (2003) *The making of modern Iran: state and society under Riza Shah, 1921–1941*, London [u.a.]: RoutledgeCurzon.

Dalton, J. R. (1994) *The Green Rainbow: Environmental Groups in Western Europe.* New Haven, CT: Yale University Press.

Daneshvar, P. (1996) *Revolution in Iran*, Basingstoke: Macmillan [u.a.].

Edmonds, R.L. (2007) 'Perspectives of Time and Change: Rethinking Embedded Environmental Activism in China', *China Information* (21): 331–44.

Ehteshami, A. (1995) *After Khomeini: The Iranian second republic*, London [u.a.]: Routledge.

Eisenstadt, S.N. (2001) 'The Civilizational Dimension of Modernity: Modernity as a Distinct Civilization', *International Sociology* 16(3):320–40.

——(2003) *Comparative civilizations & multiple modernities: a collection of essays by S.N. Eisenstadt*, Leiden [u.a.]: Brill.

——(2004) 'The Civilizational Dimension of Modernity: Modernity as a Distinct Civilization' in S. A. Arjomand and E.A. Tyryakian (eds) *Rethinking Civilizational Analysis*, London: Sage Publications.

Elton, L.D. (2001) *The history of Iran*, Westport Conn [u.a.]: Greenwood Press.

Eyerman, R. and Jamison, A. (1991) *Social Movements: A cognitive approach.* Cambridge: Polity Press.

Fadaee, S. (2011a) 'Environmental Movements in Iran: Application of the New Social Movement Theory in the Non-European Context', *Social Change* 41(1): 79–96.

——(2011b) 'Global Expansion of Capitalism, Inequality and Social Movements: The Iranian Case', in B. Rehbein (ed.) *Globalization and Inequality in Emerging Societies*, Basingstoke: Palgrave-Macmillan.

Gadgil, M. and Ramachandra, G. (1994) 'Ecological conflicts and the Environmental Movement in India', *Development and Change* (25): 101–36.

Gasiorowski, M.J. (2005) 'The 1953 Coup d'Etat Against Mosaddeq' in M.J. Gasiorowski and M. Byrne (eds) *Mohammad Mosaddeq and the 1953 Coup in Iran*, Syracuse N.Y.: Syracuse University Press.

Gellner, E. (1994) *Conditions of Liberty: Civil Society and Its Rivals*, New York, N.Y: Allen Lane/ Penguin Press.

Ghamari-Tabrizi, B. (2004) 'Contentious Public Religion: Two Conceptions of Islam in Revolutionary Iran: Ali Shariati and Abdol karim Soroush', *International Sociology* 19(4): 504–23.

Ghani, C. (1999) *Iran and the rise of Reza Shah: from Qajar collapse to Pahlavi rule*, London [u.a.]: Tauris.

Giddens, A. (1987) *Social Theory and Modern Sociology*, Stanford, Calif.: Stanford University Press.

——(1990) *The Consequences of Modernity*, Cambridge: Polity Press.

Gross, A. E. *et al.* (1983) 'The Men's Movement: Personal versus Political' in J. Freemann (ed.) *Social movements of the sixties and seventies.* New York [u.a.]: Longman.

Habermas, J. (1992) *The Structural Transformation of the Public Sphere: An Inquiry into a Category of Bourgeoisie Society*, Cambridge: Polity Press.

Hall, S. (ed.) (1996) *Modernity: An Introduction to Modern Societies*, Oxford: Blackwell.

Halliday, F. (1979) *Iran: dictatorship and development*, Harmondsworth: Penguin Books.

——(2003) 'Foreword', in A. Mohammadi (ed.) *Iran Encountering Globalization: problems and prospects*, London [u.a.]: RoutledgeCurzon.

Hashemi, N. (2004) 'The Relevance of John Lock to Social Change in the Muslim World: A Comparison with Iran', in R. Jahanbegloo (ed.) *Iran: Between Tradition and Modernity*, Lanham, MD: Lextington books.

Held, D. (2006) *Models of Democracy*, Stanford: Stanford University Press.

Hirts, D. (1997) 'Media Spins a New Image for Islam', *The Guardian* 31 March: 10.

Ho, P. and Edmonds, R.L. (2007) 'Perspectives of Time and Change: Rethinking Embedded Environmental Activism in China', *China Information* (21): 331–44.

Huntington, S. P. (1996) *The Clash of Civilizations: Remaking of World Order*, London: Simon& Schuster.

Jalaipur, H. (2003) *jameshensai-e Jonbeshhaye Ejtemai: ba takid bar jonbeshe eslhi-e dovome khordad*, Tehan: Tarheno.

Kaefeler, H. (1988) *Modernization, Legitimacy and Social Movement*, Ethnologisches Seminar der Universitaet Zürich.

Kamali, M. (2007) 'Multiple Modernities and Islamism in Iran', *Social Compass* 54(3): 373–87.

Kamrava, M. (1992) *The political history of modern Iran: from tribalism to theocracy*, Westport Conn [u.a.]: Praeger.

Kasravi, A. (2006) *History of the Iranian constitutional revolution*, Costa Mesa, Calif: Mazda Publishers, Inc.

Katouzian, H. (1981) *The Political Economy of Modern Iran*, London and New York: Macmillan and New York University Press.

——(1990) *Musaddiq and the struggle for power in Iran*, London: Tauris [u.a.].

——(2003) *Iranian history and politics: the dialectic of state and society*, London [u.a.]: RoutledgeCurzon.

Kaya, I. (2004a) *Social Theory and Later Modernities: The Turkish Experience.* Liverpool: Liverpool University Press.

——(2004b) 'Modernity, Openness, Interpretation: A Perspective on Multiple Modernities', *Social Science Information* 43(1): 35–5.

Keddie., N.R. (1981) *Roots of Revolution*, New Haven: Yale University.

——(2006) *Modern Iran: roots and results of revolution*, New haven, Conn [u.a.]: Yale University Press.

Khatami, M. (1997) 'Opening Statement at the Eight Sessions of the Islamic Summit Conference in Tehran'. Online. Available <http://president.ir/khatami/speeches/760918.htm> (accessed 15 September 2006).

Khatami, M. *et al.* (2001) *Dialogue among civilizations: a paradigm for Peace*, Pretoria: University of Pretoria.

Khiabani, G. and Sreberny, A. (2001) 'The Iranian Press and the Continuing Struggle Over Civil Society 1998–2000', *Gazette* 63(2–3): 203–23.

Khomeini, R. and Algar, H. (1981) *Islam and revolution: writings and declarations of Imam Khomeini*, Berkeley: Mizan Press.

Khosrokhavar, F. (2004) 'The Islamic Revolution in Iran: Retrospect after a Quarter of a Century', *Thesis Eleven* (76): 70–84.

Kinzer, S. (2003) *All the Shah's Men: An American Coup and the Roots of Middle East Terror*, New York: John Wiley and Sons.

Klandermans B. (1988) 'The formation and mobilization of consensus', in Klandermans B., Kriesi H., and Tarrow S. (eds) *From Structure to Action: Comparing Social Movement Research across Cultures*, Vol. 1. Greenwich, CT: JAI Press, 173–96.

Kolb, D. (1986) *The Critique of Pure Modernity: Hegel, Heidegger and After*, Chicago IL and London: University of Chicago Press.

Looney, R.E. (1982) *Economic origins of the Iranian Revolution*, New York/Frankfurt [u.a.]: Pergamon Pr.

McAdam, D. (1982) *Political process and the development of Black Insurgency*, Chicago: University of Chicago Press.

Makki, H. (1982) *Zindagani-i Mirza Taghi Han Amir-i kabir*, Tehran: Bungah-i Targuma va Nasr-i Kitab.

——(1991) *Salha-i nahdat-i milli*, Tehran: Intisarat-i Ilmi.

Martin, V. (2003) *Creating an Islamic State: Khomeini and the Making of a New Iran*, London [u.a.]: Tauris.

McCarthy, J.D. and Zald M.N. (1973) *The Trends of Social Movements in America: Professionalization and Resource Mobilization*, Morristown, N. J.: General learning Press.

Melucci, A. (1980) 'The New Social Movements: A Theoretical Approach', *Social Science Information* 19 (2): 199–226.

———(1984) 'An End to Social Movements?' Introductory Paper to the Sessions on 'New movements and Change in Organizational Forms', *Social Science Information* 23: 819–35.

———(1989) *Nomads of the Present: Social Movements and Individual Needs in Contemporary Society*, London: Hutchinson Radius.

———(1996a) *Challenging codes: collective action in the information age*, New York: Cambridge & New York: University Press.

———(1996b) 'Individual Experience and Global Issues in a Planetary Society', *Social Science Information* 35(3): 485–509.

———(1996c) *The playing self: person and meaning in the planetary society*, Cambridge & New York: Cambridge University Press.

Melucci, A. and Avritzer, L. (2000) 'Complexity, cultural pluralism and democracy: collective action in the public space', *Social Science Information* (39): 507–27.

Mir-Hosseini, Z. and Tapper R. (2006) *Islam and democracy in Iran: Eshkevari and the quest for reform*, London [u.a.]: Tauris.

Mirsepassi, A. (2000) *Intellectual discourse and the politics of modernization: negotiating modernity in Iran*, Cambridge [u.a.]: Cambridge University Press.

Mohammadi, A. (2006) 'Iran and modern media in the age of globalization', in A. Mohammadi (ed.) *Iran Encountering Globalization: problems and prospects*, London [u.a.]: RoutledgeCurzon.

Moore, B.J. (1966) *Social Origins of Dictatorship and Democracy: Lord and Peasant in the Making of the Modern World*, Boston: Beacon Press.

Mouzelis, N. (1995) 'Modernity, Late Development and Civil Society', in J. A. Hall (ed.) *Civil Society: Theory, History, Comparison*, Cambridge: Polity Press.

Morris, A.D. and Herring, C. (1987) 'Theory and research in social movements: A critical Review' in S. Long (ed.) *Annual Review of Political Science Vol. 2.* Norwood, NJ: Ablex Publishing.

Moshiri, F. (1985) *The state and social revolution in Iran: a theoretical perspective*, New York [u.a.]: Lang.

Musaddeq, M. (1988) *Musaddiq's Memoirs: The End of the British Empire in Iran*, London: JHBE for National Movement of Iran.

Nozari, I. (2001) *Tarih-i ahzab-i siyasi dar Iran, Siraz*: Intisarat-i Nawid.

Naji, K. (2008) *Ahmadinejad: The secret history of Iran's radical leader*, London [u.a.]: Tauris.

Oberschall, A. (1973) *Social conflict and social movements*, Englewood Cliffs, N.J.: Prentice-Hall.

Offe, C. (1980) 'Am Staat vorbei? Krise der Parteien und neue sozial Bewegungen', *Das Argument* 22 (124): 809–21.

———(1984) *Contradictions of the Welfare State*, London: Hutchinson.

———(1987) 'Changing Boundaries of Institutional Politics: Social Movements since the 1960s', in C.S. Maier (ed.) *Changing Boundaries of the Political*, Cambridge: Cambridge University Press.

Park, R.E. (ed.) (1967) *On social control and collective behavior: selected papers*, Chicago: The University of Chicago Press.

Parsa, M. (1989) *Social origins of the Iranian revolution*, New Brunswick [u.a.]: Rutgers University Press.

Parsons, T. (1951) *The Social System*, Glencoe, Ill.: Free Press.

——(1967) *Structure of Social Action*, Glencoe, Ill.: Free Press.

——(1982) *Essays in Sociological Theory*, New York: Free Press [u.a.].

Parsons, T. and Shills, E. A. (eds) (1951) *Toward a General Theory of Action*, Cambridge: Harvard University Press.

Payvand News Agency (2005) Available www.payvand.com (accessed 25 October 2008).

Pickvance, K. (1998) *Democracy and environmental movements in Eastern Europe: a comparative study of Hungary and Russia*, Boulder. Colo. [u.a.]: Westview Press.

Poulson, S.C. (2006) *Social Movements in Twentieth-century Iran: Culture, Ideology and Mobilizing Frameworks*, Lanham, Md.: Lexington Books.

Rahnema, A. (1998) *An Islamic Utopian: A Political Biography of Ali Shariati*, London [u.a.]: Tauris.

Razzaghi, S. (2007) *Analysis of the Status of the Iranian Civil Society: Opportunities, Challenges and Strategies*, Unpublished paper.

Rehbein, B. (2007) *Globalization, Culture and Society in Laos*, London/ New York: Routledge.

Scott, A. (1990) *Ideology and the new social movements*, London: Unwin Hyman.

——(1996) 'Movements of Modernity: Some Questions of Theory, Method and Interpretation', in J. Clarck and M. Dianni (eds) *Alain Touraine.* London and Washington, DC: Flamer Press.

Seddighi, S. (2001) 'Den Dialog fortsetzen', in S. Seddighi and B. Nirumand (eds) *Iran nach den Wahlen: Eine Konferenz und ihre Folgen*, Münster: Westfaelisches Dampfboot.

Skogen, K. (1999) 'Another Look at Culture and Nature: How Culture Patterns Influence Environmental Orientation Among Norwegian Youth', *Acta Sociologica* (42): 223–39.

Smelser, N. J. (1962) *Theory of Collective Behavior*, New York: The Free Press of Glencoe.

Smelser, N.J. and Baltes, P.B. (eds) (2001) *International Encyclopedia of the Social and Behavioral Sciences*, Amsterdam/ New York: Elsevier.

Tabari, K. (2003) 'The Rule of Law and the Politics of Reform in Post Revolutionary Ian', *International Sociology* 18(1): 96–113.

Tavakoli-Targhi, M. (2001) 'The Homeless Text of Persianate Modernity', *Cultural Dynamics* 13(3):263–91.

Tilly, C. (1984) 'Social movements and national politics', in C. Bright and S. Harding (eds) *Statemaking and social movement*, Ann Arbor: University of Michigan Press.

——(2004) *Social Movements, 1978–2004*, Boulder, CO/ London: Paradigm Publishers.

Touraine, A. (1981) *The Voice and the Eye: An Analysis of Social Movements*, Cambridge: Cambridge University Press.

——(1995) *Critique of Modernity*, Cambridge, Mass.: Blackwell.

——(1996) 'A Sociology of the Subject', in J. Clarck and M. Dianni (eds) *Alain Touraine*. London /Washington, DC: Flamer Press.

——(1997) *What is Democracy?* Boulder, Colorado: West view Press.

——(2000) *Can We Live Together?* Cambridge: Polity Press.

Tucker, K.H. (2005) 'From the Imaginary to Subjectivation: Castoriadis and Touraine on the Performative Public Sphere', *Thesis Eleven* 83(42): 42–60.

Wittrock, B. (2000) 'Modernity: One, none, or many? European origins and modernity as a global condition', *Daedalus, Journal of the American Academy of Arts and Sciences* 129(1): 31–60.

Yack, B. (1997) *The fetishism of modernities: epochal self-consciousness in contemporary social and political thought*, Notre Dame, IN: University of Notre Dame Press.

Yussfi Eshkevari, H. (2001) ' Iran nach den Wahlen', in S. Seddighi and B. Nirumand (eds) *Iran nach den Wahlen: Eine Konferenz und ihre Folgen*, Münster: Westfaelisches Dampfboot.

Yaghmaian, B. (2002) *Social change in Iran: an eyewitness account of dissent, defiance, and new movements for rights*, Albany: State University of New York Press.

Zabih, S. (1966) *The Communist movement in Iran*, Berkeley, Calif. [u.a.]: University of California Press.

Zald, M.N. and McCarthy, J.D. (1988) 'Resource mobilization and social movements: A partial theory', in M.N. Zald and J.D. McCarthy (eds) *Social Movements in an Organizational Society*, New Brunswick, NJ: Transaction, Inc.

Zibakalam, S. (2004) *Veda ba Dovome Khordad*, Tehran: Rozaneh.

Index